The wind up merchant

Brett Ellis

Dear Anna,

enjoy the book!

Brett

Introduction

Pat Keriss is the pi**taker and my alter ego. I wanted to add an element of fun to the senders of the following collection of wind up e mails by using an anagram. Pat is, in PC parlance, 'non gender specific', adding another element of mystery to the e-mails and the responses.

Having written scores of published articles but having never completed writing a book (although I am currently half way through about five), I wanted something I could dip into as and when I felt like it. The format of this book was the perfect answer to my problem of having a low boredom threshold. Thinking through my strengths I realised that I enjoy a good 'josh' and that I have undertaken some pretty good wind ups on friends and family over the years.

The problem of winding up family members is that they a) can get very sensitive/ offended, b) The recipient can become seriously embarrassed, and most importantly c) the loss of pride dictates the seeking of retribution. Vengeance never sleeps and having your friends and family close, even for years after you have wound them up, will lead to you getting a large dose of your own medicine either tomorrow, next week or in twenty years time.

Originally, the e-mails sent were intended to be aimed at companies and individuals that I believe deserve vitriol and embarrassment. That intention changed however to include those that I believe would take the wind ups as intended...as a joke. Some companies targeted I have felt let down by or I feel have taken themselves far too seriously in the past. Some others I believe have 'misled' customers by overcharging or producing sub standard products or services that I see as a con.

Some e-mails I have felt embarrassed to send. A few I have deleted. A few I feel ashamed to have sent including the majority of those to small businesses who are trying to but make a crust. Apologies in advance for any offence I have caused...I just hope you can see the attempted funny side of my prose in the cold light of day.

All e mails, and their Reponses, were sent over a 3 month period. The biggest disappointment has been the lack of responses from a number of companies. I dallied with the idea of not including the non response e-mails in this book but decided against it as, I like to think, a large proportion of the humour in the book is not just in the responses.

You may form the impression that there is a lot of hatred in my writings and, to be fair, with some, there is. I despise officialdom and the holier than thou approach of big business who are prepared to preach but not to practice. Tesco for example can train their staff to ask me to bring my own carrier bags to take home my shopping. In principle I agree whole heartedly. In practice though, a company that has ruined swathes of small shopkeepers, makes huge profits and who do not run their stores or trucks on solar or 'green' power, do not have the right to tell me what vessels I should use in which to pack my shopping.

It is the hypocrisy that appals me, but in our society we are either brainwashed or scared into keeping quiet so that we do not complain. With this approach I am trying to redress the balance by at least causing some kind of minor embarrassment.

All e-mails have not been doctored in any way at all. What you read is exactly how it is. Some responses have put a huge smile on my face, particularly from smaller businesses. The larger businesses have not failed either due to the seriousness of their responses to what are quite frankly ridiculous queries.

My motivation for writing this book? Well, I have to have a mission and for a series of months this has been it, also, I would love this to be a success and throw it out there to see how it fairs. Your views whether negative or otherwise will be greatly appreciated and I will still be checking Pat's e mail address once in a while if you want to drop me a line: patkeriss@yahoo.co.uk

OK. Intro over....time to take the pi**........

Brett Ellis
Copyright © Brett Ellis 2010

Contents:

Number:	Title:
1	Car wax
2	Boots
3	Rastafari
4	B-Ball
5	Shit in pasty
6	Massive bender
7	Pubic clothing
8	The habit
9	Blinding incompetence
10	A cut below
11	Linguistic fantastic
12	The white stuff
13	Mini wind up
14	Mile high club
15	MNASEQI
16	One big happy family
17	Cruising for a bruising
18	Pole prance
19	Cold comfort
20	Lady hermaphrodite
21	Pussy burn
22	Blown tyre
23	Barking
24	Mild green
25	The great indoors
26	A common stamp
27	Toy story
28	To the wall
29	Long pot
30	Candle vandal
31	TV times
32	Cleaning up
33	Hanna barbera
34	A load of old pony
35	Man's best friend
36	A sticky situation
37	Plastic tragitastic
38	Downsizing

39	Crowning glory
40	Causing a stink
41	Spoken
42	Glue
43	Shapely soaker
44	Wodka hell
45	Sonnet
46	It's a fair cop
47	Sheathing environmentalists
48	Norway is that a new car
49	Toffee crumble
50	A balls up
51	Fragrant vagrant
52	Free the meat
53	A little bit of jazz
54	Cock of the century
55	It's going to be huge
56	A close shave
57	Meow
58	Cheesemonger
59	Feeling ruff
60	Chin chin
61	Well travelled
62	Pride of the north
63	Feck that
64	Glamping
65	Meatfeast
66	Softly does it
67	Bouncy bouncy
68	Off the scale
69	Roper
70	Hoarhouse
71	It'll cost ya
72	Party time
73	Feeling sheepish
74	Errol
75	What a wanker
76	Sure got a perdy mouth aint he?
77	A huge joke
78	Overpaid underworked planks
79	Shit off a shovel

80	Easy Rider
81	Wtf
82	Hound dog
83	Tweet tweet bang
84	Van Goch
85	Isn't that a peach?
86	Crap hole
87	Shergar's last stand
88	Custard creamed
89	Bolt from the blue
90	Give peas a chance
91	Feeling hothothot
92	Charlotte
93	Feeling chuffed
94	Beyonce
95	Slyxdexic
96	Smoking a fag
97	Catpack furniture
98	Compact risk
99	Only a squid?
100	Rough diver
101	Paul Scholes
102	Stalin
103	Puss
104	Corporate loop us
105	No place like groan
106	Throwing in the trowel
107	The calf mince
108	Something for the wick end
109	Taking the pistachio
110	Rushdie
111	Night time curlew
112	Last post
113	Dentist chair
114	You gander
115	Twocking hell
116	Transparent
117	Wee Jimmy Krankie
118	Rocket man
119	Because
120	Turn it up to 11

121	Pomp and ceremony
122	Pit pony
123	Feeling dogmatic
124	Julio
125	Eartha Kitt
126	Kerb crawler
127	Au natural
128	Dennis
129	Billy big bullocks
130	Hairy strikers
131	AM/FM
132	Tool
133	Smokey and the bandit
134	5-3?
135	Big dope
136	Albert
137	Slippery
138	Sleazy listening
139	Headroom
140	Stitch up
141	Plastic fantastic
142	House of horrors
143	No positives
144	Scraping the misery barrel
145	Pleasurable yank
146	Griffin
147	Uphill gardener
148	d.i.v.o.r.c.e
149	Taking it up the glitter
150	Felix
151	Grus 2
152	Arf arf
153	Cull em' Jamie
154	R Tards
155	Painters in
156	Big tissue
157	Pinhead
158	Jules Rimet
159	Boreham
160	Persian
161	Environ mental

1. Car wax

From: Pat Keriss
To: Car plan care (automotive@tetrosyl.com)
Subject: Wax

I would like an urgent explanation please...

Prior to a colleague's engagement party last Friday, I ran out of hair wax to use to sculpt my hair. I hastily searched my garage and found some of your CarPlan triplewax.

Obviously, the term 'wax', applies to not only cars, but to hair to keep it shiny. I applied said wax and have thus far been unable to wash it from hair despite around 20 applications of Pantene Shampoo.

I would therefore like you to explain:

a) Why the container does not contain a warning not to apply to hair, and
b) How to wash the bloody stuff out. It is extremely slippery and causing no end of problems with regard to ruining my silk pillowcases.

I would appreciate a speedy and conclusive reply

P.Keriss

From: Triplewax
To: Pat Keriss
Subject: Wax

Hi Pat, Regarding the email, about our Car Shampoo, It is A SHAMPOO FOR CARS, which it states on the bottle.

Thank You.....

From: Pat Keriss
To: Triplewax
Subject: wax

I am a dyslexic.

You really should put a picture of a person using it on their hair with a big 'no entry' sign on it.

You have acted extremely irresponsibly in this matter.

I don't even have a car. What about my money back then??

Pat

2. Boots

From: Pat Keriss
To: pharmacist@pharmacy.boots.com
Subject: Footwear

I have lived in rural Cornwall all of my life and had never, until last week had the misfortune to visit 'Boots'.

Obviously, using a pony and trap as my only form of transportation, travelling 25 miles to the nearest town was going to be hard not only on myself, but on Dobber, my faithful pony.

I am still shaking with anger with what happened once I found the 'Boots' store I had travelled so far to visit. Upon entering, I realised that you do not sell 'Boots', or, come to that, any footwear whatsoever.

I am considering contacting the authorities to have you investigated under trade descriptions. In the interim however, I demand an explanation as to why 'Boots' do not sell 'Boots'??

P. Keriss

NO RESPONSE

3. Rastafari

From: Pat Keriss
To: helpline@defra.gsi.gov.uk
Subject: Defra

I am a deaf Rastafarian. Please can you inform me as to what help is available to me through Defra?

P. Keriss

**From: DEFRA
To: Pat Keriss
Subject: DEFRA help**

Hello Pat

**Please can you elaborate on the type of assistance you require and we can then deal with your e-mail accordingly.
Many thanks
Defra Helpline**

From: Pat Keriss
To: DEFRA
Subject: DEFRA help

I would have thought that would be self explanatory. I am deaf and a Rastafarian. You are defra, the deaf Rastafarian charity...what can you offer me in my predicament?

Regards

P. Keriss

**From: DEFRA
To: Pat Keriss
Subject: DEFRA help**

**Dear Pat
I'm really sorry, Defra is not a charity for the deaf and we are therefore unable to assist you in this instance.
With kind regards**
Defra Helpline

4. B-Ball

From: Pat Keriss
To: British Basketball Association (BBAUK)
Subject: Travellers

I am a Romany Gipsy. Upon playing Basketball for the first time last week, I was told it was an offence to travel, or be a traveller and that this offence is sanctioned by the BBA.

How dare you deem it an offence to be a traveller and use this to penalise someone whilst playing the game of basketball. I believe this to be racist and demand an urgent explanation.

P. Keriss

NO RESPONSE

5. Shit in Pastry

From: Pat Keriss
To: Ginsters
Subject: Meat

I have been an avid fan of Ginsters Cornish pasties for many years. I adore the taste, texture and the taste explosion as it first hits the gullet. For me, it is better than any feeling I have ever experienced in life thus far.

I was shocked however yesterday. I purchased a pastie for lunch and to my extreme surprise, I found a lump of real meat in the said pasty.

Please can you explain adequately how a Ginsters pasty came to have some real meat inside it? I would also like a written assurance that this will never happen again.

I look forward to your reply.

P. Keriss

From: Ginsters
To: Pat Keriss
Subject: Meat

Dear Ms Keriss

Thank you for your email and may I apologise for us not responding to your original e-mail.

A letter is on its way to you in today's post, together with some vouchers.

Kind regards

Caroline Sheppard
Customer Services
Ginsters

6. Massive Bender

From: Pat Keriss
To: Uri Geller
Subject: Quiz quandary

Hi Uri

I make my living from the use of a number of quiz machines in pubs and amusement arcades.

Recently, I was on the 'cash splash' section of such a game and a question came up for which I was told I was wrong and thus, lost my pot of money.

Obviously I am very upset about this and I would like to take the machine makers to task and reclaim lost winnings. I am hoping you can help...

The question was 'is Uri Geller a bender'?

Obviously, knowing you are married, I hit 'no'. This answer was marked wrong.

Please could you clear up this matter so that I can take this matter further?

Many thanks and keep up the good work.

Pat

NO RESPONSE

7. Pubic clothing

From: Pat Keriss
To: Wayne Hemingway
Subject: Winter warmer range

Hi Wayne,

I've been a fan of yours for years and have a proposition for you.....

I have designed a range of clothing using different colours and styles of human hair. I have skirts, dresses, coats and even socks which are designed and manufactured by myself.

I bind the hair (head, pubic and body) together using a (patent pending) solution I have devised. I have been wearing my designs for 2 winters now and, despite initial problems with regard to itching on the skin, I have been amazed by the complimentary comments I have received from friends and strangers alike.

I would like to invite you to partner me in this project and put the Hemingway stamp of approval on my 'winter warmer' range.

I am sure you will be interested and look forward to meeting you in the near future.

Please let me know when you would like to meet. Bear in mind Tuesday afternoons are not good for me as I have to attend an ADHD support group.

Much love

Pat

**From: Wayne Hemingway
To: Pat Keriss
Subject: Winter warmer range**

very interesting , but not for us   ....and we wish you success!!

From: Pat Keriss
To: Wayne Hemingway
Subject: Winter warmer range

You really are missing out on the chance of a lifetime. You could leave your loved ones as the 'hair' to a global brand (excuse the pun). No wonder red or dead ended up as the latter.

P.Keriss

8. The habit

From: Pat Keriss
To: Nicotinell.co.uk
Subject: Plasters

I was recently at my friend's house playing bat and ball. I slipped on the concrete and cut my knee quite badly. Upon looking for some plasters, my friend could only find Nicotinell patches. I placed a patch on my wound and it stopped the blood flow.

The next morning, after taking off the patch/ plaster however I felt very strange. After breakfast I subconsciously picked up a packet of cigarettes and smoke three back to back. I am 36 and have never smoked in my life.

I believe placing the patch on my knee has now giving me a cigarette habit that I never had prior to putting on your plaster/ patch.

Please can you inform me as to what you intend to do to rectify this situation as I am now smoking 50 a day and cannot play bat and ball anymore without wheezing like an asthmatic?

From: Nicotinell
To: Pat Keriss
Subject: Nicotinell patch: Unlicensed use

Dear Pat Keriss

Thank you for your email to the Nicotinell website.

As clearly stated, both on the Nicotinell pack and on the patient information inside, Nicotinell patches are an aid to stop smoking and are not for use by non-smokers. Using the product over a cut on your knee is therefore considered an inappropriate use and outside of our license for the product. Help with stopping smoking can be sought from your General Practitioner or local stop smoking advisor, see:
http://smokefree.nhs.uk/?WT.mc_id=search&gclid=CMf10

9-G2JwCFUYA4wod0VVCKQ for more information.

Novartis is legally obliged to request follow up information when we receive reports such as yours. I would therefore be very grateful if you could complete the attached questionnaire and return this to me either electronically or to the Freepost address below.

If you have consulted your doctor regarding your single use of Nicotinell patch and you would be happy for Novartis to contact them for any additional information they may be able to provide please could you also sign the attached medical consent form and return the original signed copy to me at the Freepost address below.

Novartis Consumer Health
Medical Affairs Department
FREEPOST RCC 2686
Horsham
RH12 5BR

Kind regards

Medical Affairs Department
Novartis Consumer Health

From: Pat Keriss
To: Nicotinell
Subject: Nicotinell patch: unlicensed use

Dear Novaris,

Thankyou for your reply which is appreciated, although a little slow and cumbersome. I have smoked around 100 cigarettes since I sent my original mail and this situation is becoming intolerable.

I have just been to the little boys room for the thirtieth time today to 'clear my throat' in the wash basin (which is failing to impress my partner as it leaves a sticky green/ brown residue only movable when dried with a tepidly sharp object, such a quality dining fork).

Let me make this situation clear....when a person is injured playing 'bat and ball', or any other extreme sport, and they suffer a serious (if not life threatening) injury as I did to my knee, and they are offered medical assistance by a friend/ passer by/ stranger (in this case my close friend Quentin), they do not ask to see the pack and enclosed patient information! If this product is dangerous, why is it not issued under prescription?

To ask me to answer the questionnaire does not help my recently acquired, serious smoking habit. I find it intrusive and beneficial only to you. No doubt you use this information to sell my details to third parties such as Benson and Hedges or Rizla? I therefore refuse to sign this as I believe this could jeopardize any possible future compensation claim.

I am quite happy to send you a mucus sample however, as long as my DNA is not sold to any third parties. If you require this, please let me know and I will produce a document for you to sign to agree not to pass said mucus on to any third parties. I will send this recorded delivery in a plastic see through container if you wish...possibly a small Tupperware tub?

The problem still remains however and requires a resolution. Please inform me as to your next course of action to assist me. For example, do you not have an anti serum to counteract the poisonous effects of your addictive patches?

P. Keriss

From: Nicotinell
To: Pat Keriss
Subject: Nicotinell patch: Unlicensed use

Dear Pat Keriss

Thank you for your further email regarding Nicotinell patches.

The first step in all cases reported to Novartis Consumer Health of this nature is to request completion of our Medical Questionnaire, and to request medical consent to contact your doctor.

Without this information it is not possible for Novartis Consumer Health to consider this matter further. Please be assured that all information received will be treated anonymously in line with the data protection act and our disclaimer to this effect is given below:

Novartis Consumer Health UK Ltd (NCH) may process your personal data for specific and limited purposes according to the Data Protection Act 1998. Personal data is kept only for as long as necessary. NCH is committed to protecting the security of your personal data from unauthorized access, use, or disclosure. Novartis may transfer your data outside the UK or Republic of Ireland. We will ensure that all transfers are adequately protected and comply with recognized international standards. If you do not consent to your personal data being processed or for more information about the NCH Privacy Policy, please contact us or alternatively log on to our website at
http://www.novartis.co.uk/general/privacy_policy.shtml.

I have attached copies of the medical questionnaire and medical consent form again and look forward to receiving the completed forms.

Kind regards

Medical Information Department
Novartis Consumer Health

9. Blinding incompetence

From: Pat Keriss
To: Dolland and Aitchison
Subject: Contact lenses

I was recently given some 1 day contact lenses to try out. I tried, but couldn't get used to them so decided to stick to my spectacles.

My cat, Hercules, however is now aged 19 (92 in human years) and has suffered from poor eyesight for some time. I decided to therefore put a pair of contacts in Hercules eyes to aid his onset into old age. This had catastrophic results. After clawing me, he ran into a wall and jumped through an open window onto the street 2 floors below.

Sadly, after a couple of hours I took him to the vet who said that nothing could be done and he put him down.

I have now lost the only companionship I have and would like a full explanation as to why your contact lenses don't carry a warning as to why they cannot be used on pets such as Hercules?

If your response is unsatisfactory, I will be petitioning my local MP with a view to this being made compulsory.

From: Boots opticians
To: Pat Keriss
Subject: Complaint

Dear Mr. Keriss,

Thank you for your email.
After an exhaustive search of our records here at head office and at our Hastings Branch, we can find no record of having supplied you with contact lenses. If you are confident that it was a D&A practice who supplied you with your lenses, please provide further details of the location of the Branch and dates of your visits.

Also, if you have changed your name or if you may provide a different name when you attended, this information would also be useful as we have no patient by the name of Keriss with the initial P on our records.
Yours Sincerely, Darren , D&A Customer Care

From: Pat Keriss
To: Boots opticians
Subject: Complaint

Dear Darren,

Firstly, not everyone with the name 'Pat' is male. The contact lenses were handed out by one of your assistants from a drawer as a trial...you do not have a copy of my details.

This does not change the predicament that Hercules found himself in.

I would prefer to not be fobbed off and at this juncture, I demand the truth. Can you handle the truth?

P.Keriss

From: Boots
To: Pat Keriss
Subject: complaint

Dear P Keriss,

Thank you for your response.

I am aware that Pat may be a male or female name, which is why I referred to your original email where you had chosen the title 'Mr.' in your correspondence and addressed you accordingly. I did, however, search our database by both sexes and I was still not able to find anyone on our records by the name given.

I can assure you that I am not trying to fob you off, I am stating that I would like to investigate the matter, but to do this I will need to find out which D&A Branch you visited. Your complaint is concerned with the advice given to you when the lenses were provided to you.

At D&A we provide contact lens trials, but to have a trial a consultation is required to take place and we would need to record your details in this appointment. Contact lenses are prescribed items so your statement that you did not provide your details and that some lenses were just handed to you is of concern to me and I would certainly like to investigate this and the advice given to you about their wear with the Branch in question. Therefore, I require further information from you so that I can establish which Branch you visited and which colleague served you.

Please respond with any further information about when and where you visited one of our Branches so that I can respond further. I assure you that this matter will be investigated once you provide me with further details. I can also assure you that I can indeed handle the truth, whatever the truth of this matter turns out to be.

Kind regards,
Darren
D&A Customer Care

From: Pat Keriss
To: Boots
Subject: Complaint

Dear Darren,

I prefer not to pigeonhole myself as 'gender specific' for personal reasons that are known only to me and a greater power. I did indeed put 'Mr' as this is a * field on your website. I could have easily put 'third gender', 'hybrid' or 'trans' if your company was open minded enough to allow such offerings. As we are on the topic, what would you expect a hermaphrodite to put in the 'title' field? Jamie Lee Curtis, Castor Semenya or Nicole Kidman (all alleged) are apparently sufferers yet the media seem determined to classify them as 'female' which I am sure you will agree is unfair to them and their families.

I am openly paranoid about sharing intimate and personal information and must admit to telling a 'mistruth' with regard to my contact lens trial.

I used a falsified name. From memory, I believe I used the name Tony Hancock. I was in the store for around half an hour and this occurred between January and July of this year which should be specific enough for you.

Also try other 'aliases' I go under including Bill Baggins, Eddie Edwards and Tabatha Kwai.

I must take issue at this juncture with your comment 'whatever the truth of this matter turns out to be'. This could be seen as libellous, and possibly slanderous if you have repeated your comment to others.
I am only concerned with my dear Hercules and I find your implication hurtful both on an emotional and paternal/maternal level. Once the 'truth outs', I would expect a retraction of this implied implication.

I look forward to your response using the names given. Also, try Romeo Windrush if you cannot find a record for Tony, Bill, Eddie or Tabatha.

P. Keriss

From: Boots
To: Pat Keriss
Subject: complaint

Dear P Keriss,

Thank you for your further email.

I regret that I am still unable to verify that you have been provided with contact lenses by a D&A branch. Please reply providing the name which you provided to us. You will also have been asked for an address and a date of birth, both of which will have been required for your clinical record and lenses would not have been provided without this information. Please also confirm the location of the branch that you visited. If we receive these specific further details from you, rather than a range of possibilities, we will endeavour to investigate the matter.

However, unless this is provided, I regret that we will not be able to investigate, or to respond to any further emails from you on this subject.

Kind regards,
Darren
D&A Customer Care

10. A cut below

From: Pat Keriss
To: Nicky Clarke hairdressing products
Subject: Clippers

I recently bought Nicky Clarke clippers for my hair.

I have shaved my head a few times with this, as well as my body hair, which can become somewhat unmanageable at times, especially on my back and around my genitalia.

Recently, I used the trimmer to shave my pubic region. I was left after a few strokes writhing in agony after one of the blades caught the skin on my left testicle and caused a cut, and subsequent trickle of blood to run down my leg.

The bleeding continued for an hour and, in addition to the obvious discomfort, ruined a pair of white cotton linen trousers I put on for a date that evening. Suffice to say, I never saw the lady again once I informed her as to the cause of the red patch on my attire.

I would like to send the trimmers back and be issued with a replacement as I believe they are faulty. Also, I believe that I am owed £50 for the trousers and £75 for the wasted meal I paid for on the date.

Please can you agree to pay these monies so that I can forward my address details for payment?

Regards

Pat Keriss

From: Anne Holme (Pulse.co.uk)
To: Pat Keriss
Subject: Clippers

Good Afternoon,

While not specifically stating that you cannot use these clippers for the genitalia area, they only give directions for styling the hair.

This is what they were designed for and the only place they should be used.

While we sympathise with your situation we cannot be held responsible for the misuse of our products.

We are sorry for the inconvenience caused.

From: Pat Keriss
To: Anne Holme (Pulse.co.uk)
Subject: Clippers

Ann,

Most people DO have hair on the genital region (unless they suffer from Alopecia Totalia or they wax to form a Brazilian or such style).

Simply put, your products MUST include a warning to users that they should not be used on the genitalia whatsoever.

If you are so 'sorry for the inconvenience caused', then I would expect a goodwill payment to be made to cover the cost of the doomed date.

I can send you the blood stained trousers as a receipt if needed?

Pat Keriss

From: Pulse.co.uk
To: Pat Keriss
Subject: Clippers

Good Morning,

Sorry but as stated below we do not compensate for misuse.

With Regards
Customer Services

11. Linguistic fantastic

From: Pat Keriss
To: Plain English campaign
Subject: Assistance

I would like to offer my support to your worthwhile campaign.

I am getting fucked off with reading ridiculous signs and shitty jargon from companies and those pricks in the Government alike.

I would love to offer my support, preferably by use of my skills of the written word to teach these arseholes that there is no need for the bullshit they keep feeding us and to let them know we are intelligent fucking human beings.

Please let me know how I can be of assistance with anything you deem fit regarding these tossers and their wanky ways with words.

Bollocks to the corporates. Ballbags to the government. Long live the plain English campaign!

Pat

From: Tony Maher (Plain English campaign)
To: Pat Keriss
Subject: Assistance

Dear Pat

Thank you for your support.

If I can think of any way you can help, I will let you know.

All the best

Tony Maher
Manager

From: Pat Keriss
To: Tony Meher (Plain English campaign)
Subject: Assistance

Dear Tony,

That's fucking ace.

Cheers

P.Keriss

12. The white stuff

From: Pat Keriss
To: Whites estate agents (Northampton)
Subject: whites only

I can't believe in this day and age you only employ white estate agents. It is an absolute disgrace!

I am mixed race and would love a career in estate agency. My chin hit the floor when I saw the name of your estate agents. The apartheid regime ended in South Africa in 1994, yet is still alive and well in Northampton.

I believe you need to undergo a course on 'positive discrimination' in order to come into line with the rest of the western world.

Again, I am shocked and distressed that this still goes on.

Shame on you.

Pat Keriss

NO RESPONSE

13. Mini wind up

From: Pat Keriss
To: Mini motor company
Subject: production levels

I saw the headline on the yahoo homage earlier and it left me concerned.

The heading read 'Two new mini's to be built in UK'.

With the problems encountered in the UK car industry I am shocked that you are producing only 2 cars. Presumably these will go to the highest bidder?

I myself am interested in buying a new mini in the future, once I manage to get a job and save up some money. To know I will not be able to as you are only making 2 of them is a disgrace.

I have been a long time supporter of everything produced in Britain. If this is your attitude toward potential customers though, I will be buying Chinese from here on in.

Pat Keriss

To: Pat Keriss
From: Mini motor company
Subject: Production levels

Dear Sir or Madam

Thank you for your email to MINI Customer Information.

I am very glad that you decided to write to us as it does expose the problems that headlines can create. This is true whether the headlines are newspaper headlines or on the internet.

Headlines are created to attract customers and/or readers and can, as in this case, seem to give slightly wrong information.

The correct information is that there are two new models of the MINI being created at the MINI Plant in Oxford.

This means that there will be lots of each new model built and this should mean that there will be one available for you also when you are in a position to think about getting one.

I trust this information is useful but please do not hesitate to contact me should you have any further queries.

Yours faithfully

MINI UK
Elfriede McNeal
Customer Information Advisor

From: Pat Keriss
To: Mini car company
Subject: production levels

Now I am confused as I believe you are contradicting yourself and telling mistruths to potential customers! (me).

You firstly say that there are 'two new models of MINI being created'. You then say there will be 'lots' of them being built. It can't be both! It's either two cars, or lots of cars. Also, how many is 'lots'? 20? 30? Maybe even 50?

Please tell me the truth or my hard earned future savings will be lining the pockets of some 'smart' car people instead if you catch my drift....

P. Keriss

From: Mini
To: Pat Keriss
Subject: Production levels

Dear P. Keriss

Thank you for your reply.

I am sorry you feel we are not telling you the truth regarding the two new MINI models, however, I think you may have misunderstood my colleagues email and the press report.

Two new models of MINI are being created. We currently have three models available, the Hatchback, Clubman and Convertible. Two exciting new models will be added to the line up in the near future, and manufactured at our factory in Oxford – taking our model range to 5 vehicle types. We currently manufacture around 250,000 MINIs per year at this factory, and this figure is made up of the Hatchback, Clubman and Convertible.

So to summarise, two new models are being created, and lots of examples of those two models will be built at Plant Oxford.

I hope this explains the situation further, however, please do contact me should you require any further clarification.

Yours sincerely

MINI UK
Christian Gorton
Customer Information Advisor

From: Pat Keriss
To: Mini
Subject: Production levels

I think I am now clear....

You have five different types of mini on sale?
You make 250,000 of three of the types?

You are only making 'examples' of the two new types?

If this is the case, are you using the examples to sell the only two 'real, finished versions' you are producing of the new two types?

Why not make 250,000 real cars instead of just making examples?

Seems pretty silly to me and I now see why the dominance of the British car industry is being challenged from other countries with a proud tradition of making (more than 2!) cars such as Vietnam and Cuba.

How can you justify making tens of thousands of examples to result in the selling of just two cars? The world's gone mad.

P. Keriss

From: Mini
To: Pat Keriss
Subject: Production levels

Dear P. Keriss

Thank you for your reply.

Three different of types of MINI are currently for sale, and an additional 2 or 3 will be added in the coming years.

We produce 250,000 cars per year, made up from the current 3 car model range - the Hatchback, Clubman and Convertible.

By stating we are making examples of these vehicles, I do mean the finished product that we sell. I used the word example as only 2 in every 100,000 cars are built with the same options – they don't all look the same even if they are from the same model line.

We could never make only two of any vehicle, as we could not survive on such a low income unless those cars sold for hundreds of millions each!

So to summarise, MINI manufactures and sells approximately 250,000 cars per year. This is currently made up from 3 model lines. In the future, we expect to manufacture and sell more than 250,000 cars per year as we will add more vehicles to the MINI model line up.

Please contact me should you have any further questions.

Yours sincerely

MINI UK
Christian Gorton
Customer Information Advisor

14. Mile high club

From: Pat Keriss:
To: British Airways
Subject: Aviator

I have recently set up my own adult film business from my base in Essex. Basically I have a proposition for you which could help to fill first class on one of your flights...

I would like to film an adult film on a scheduled flight booking all of the first class seats (for a mates rate/ block booking discount of around 70% if possible)?

I will be bringing along 16 experienced adult actors for a film entitled 'the shave he ate her'. (This is a clever play on words for the 'Aviator').

The actors will, as part of a complex and thought provoking 'romcom' story eventually capitulate and become extremely intimate with each other.

I have my basic food hygiene and health safety certificates (level one) so I will be able to clear up any mess/ stains etc should they occur.

The filming should take approximately 3 hours and will include some loving scenes of penetrative sex, both front and back 'door'. These will be tasteful and our aim is to have our runner holding the curtain shut at all times in order to avoid the voyeurs in club class.

Please let me know what date is good for you so that I can undertake a booking.

Many thanks

Pat Keriss

p.s. Would it be possible to borrow a couple of captain's uniforms for the duration of the filming?

From: British Airways
To: Pat Keriss
Subject: Aviator

Dear Mr Keriss

I am sorry we are unable to help with your specific request by email.

Please contact our local sales office, where one of our agents will be able to assist you. Their telephone numbers, addresses and opening times can be found at:

http://www.britishairways.com/travel/ctclist

I hope this helps and thank you for your email.

Regards
Sufiya
British Airways

15. MNASEQI

From: Pat Keriss
To: MENSA
Subject: IQ

I dun a iq tesst last wek. I dun ok geting scorr of 80 not fra frm bein genis. howw kan I gett beter to gett 150 ? fanks.

NO RESPONSE

16. One big happy family

To: Muslim council of Britain
From: Pat Keriss
Subject: Blessing

Hi,

I am sick and tired of all the bad press toward Islam with regard to most aspects of your religion, including that of the Muslim view (as reported by the press) toward homosexuality.

I would like to propose something that might help to redress the balance....

I would like to undertake a blessing in one of your communal buildings to bless my partnership with my boyfriend/ common law husband, David.

We have been together for a number of years and are deeply in love. I would like to not only declare this love to the world, but also show that your faith is accepting of all, including homosexuals/ old queens like myself!

We just require the use of a building for a couple of hours. We will be having a small, but intimate gathering afterwards at our house with nibbles (finger buffet/ cheese and pineapple on sticks) and some quality music (Pet shop boys, Scissor Sisters et al...). You will of course be more than welcome to join us.

Please let me know if you are agreeable (as I am sure you will be).

Much Love

(Mr) P. Keriss

NO RESPONSE

17. Cruising for a bruising

From: Pat Keriss
To: Somali tourist board
Subject: Cruise

Hi,

I am interested, along with my wife, in taking a relaxing cruise along the coast of Somalia. We are looking forward to putting our feet up, enjoying some stunning scenery and meeting the friendly locals. We have also head of your Pirates of the Caribbean theme cruises which sound like a treat! Please could you forward me the details of any companies that offer cruises?

Many thanks

Pat Keriss

NO RESPONSE

18. Pole prancer

From: Pat Keriss
To: Peter Stringfellow
Subject: PDP

Hi Peter....

I would like to give you the opportunity to meet me with my new product design which I am sure you will want to order. It is a unique piece of contemporary sculpture which will blow your competitors out of the water!

I have designed a PDP (pole dance phallus) (Not to be confused with the PSP which is something different altogether).

It is a pole with brass phalluses welded on at 6 inch intervals up the length. The phallus is copper coated. The idea is simple...as your dancer gyrates up the pole, she can use the phallus to sit on and tease her genitalia in order to give the customers a really intimate view of her vaginal region. This is turn will lead to higher tips, and hence, more profit for you!

The pole is lubricant resistant and I will offer a 2 year anti rust guarantee on each purchase.

Please let me know when you would be available to watch a demonstration of the PDP.

By the way...It can also be used by male dancers. Please state a preference as to whether you would prefer my wife Anita, or myself to demo dance for you using the PDP?

Much love

Pat

NO RESPONSE

<u>19. Cold comfort</u>

From: Pat Keriss
To: Selfridges
Subject: Budweiser mini fridge

I have been after a 'Budweiser 12" AS33454 mini fridge' with temperate climate control and backdraft facility for a while. This model, as I am sure you are aware being purveyors of fridges, also offers the tepid cooling system (TCS) and High J movement control (HJMC).

I would prefer the colour to be metallic gung ho green, but will settle for the finefin yellow snowflake option at a push.

Please can you tell me how much this model costs including delivery and the likely delivery date?

P. Keriss

From: Selfridges
To: Pat Keriss
Subject: Budweiser mini fridge

Thank you for your recent email in regards to Fridges.

Unfortunately we do not stock any large white electrical goods within Selfridges.

I am sorry we could not assist you further.

Thank you for taking the time to contact Selfridges.

Regards

Charlotte

From: Pat Keriss
To: Selfridges
Subject: Budweiser mini fridge

I am not sure if you are taking the rise out of me?

The clue is in the name. Sel fridges sel fridges. Hardly rocket science I'm sure you'll concur?

Please can you pass me onto someone who can discuss my enquiry regarding the AS33454 as a matter of urgency? I have a FAST (Fridge appreciation society team) meeting next month and I would dearly love to impress my peers with one of the most revered cold storage devices known to man.

I have a friend with a trailer so can collect if you can arrange around £7 to cover his petrol and sundry expenses.

P.Keriss

20. Lady Hermaphrodite

From: Pat Keriss
To: Prince Michael of Kent
Subject: Studies

I am currently studying at a college in South London and writing an article on hermaphrodites. I heard that, along with Jamie Lee Curtis and Nicole Kidman, either you or your wife (I forget which Michael?) is rumoured to suffer from this affliction?

Please could you verify for the purposes of my studies whether this is true? If it is, would you mind answering a brief written q and a session with me over the next week?

Many thanks.

NO RESPONSE

21. Pussy burn

From: Pat Keriss
To: Deep heat
Subject: deep heat

I recently purchased some deep heat for my toe which has caused me some discomfort after I dropped a clothes iron on it from 5 foot.

I put a large lump on my toe when barefoot to alleviate the pain. Last week however, my cat sat on my toe. Inadvertently the cat managed to get a lump of deep heat around its anal region. This caused it severe discomfort and it went what I can only describe as 'spastic'.

Anyhow, he tried to wipe it by hurling his hind legs over his front and rubbing his anus region on our tiled floor. This made the situation worse and he rubbed the deep heat in more, causing him even more discomfort.

He then attempted to lick it off his anus. Having got the deep heat on his lips he started frothing at the mouth as he whizzed around the floor.

To cut to the quick, he is now hiding under a kitchen unit and refuses to come out and eat or drink. He has urinated and passed motions under the cabinet and as well as the effect of the smell for me, I am concerned about his nutritional and emotional well being.

You must have experienced this problem before.

What do you suggest (as a matter of urgency) that I do?

Many thanks in advance.

P. Keriss

From: Deep Heat
To: Pat Keriss
Subject: deep heat

Dear Mr Keriss

I refer to your recent, and somewhat distressing, email concerning a misadventure between Deep Heat Rub and your cat's bottom. Contrary to your suggestion, this is in fact the first time I've encountered such a scenario!

The product contains 4 active ingredients, all of which have the effect of generating warmth on the skin in humans. Whilst it has never been tested on animals, it is very likely that the same effect will be experienced by a cat and that the sensation will be exaggerated on the most sensitive areas of the body such as the anus. It is for this reason that application of the cream to these locations is to be avoided in humans.

No doubt your cat experienced some discomfort and psychological distress at the time, not least for being unable to explain the reason for such an unwanted sensation. In addition, cats are known to have some sensitivity towards aspirin - Deep Heat Rub contains an aspirin-like drug known as salicylic acid. It is very likely however that, in such small doses encountered by the transfer of cream from your foot, any ill effects will have been transient and will (no doubt) have passed by the time you receive this response.

As will all cases of animal ill health, I would suggest that your best course of action is to consult your vet to be sure that no lasting effects have resulted. He may wish to carry out some checks, although a cat scan is unlikely! I'm confident that the worst your pet will have experienced - other than the initial distress - will have been a reduction in the number of lives that it has as its disposal. I hope that this news is comforting and reassuring to you.
Regards
Colin Brown/ Lydsey Pollock
Director of Research & Quality Development The Mentholatum Company Limited UK

From: Pat Keriss
To: Lyndsey Pollock(Deep heat)
Subject: Deep heat

Dear Ms Pollock,

I trust your response is genuine....your name sounds a bit fishy to me..?

I am surprised you have not encountered such a scenario? Surely there must be similar situations where, for example, a man has inadvertently scratched his 'gentleman bits' and has experienced some level of discomfort?

There has been some movement thankfully with regard to Hercules. He has come to the gap in the kitchen unit and has taken on board some solids and liquids. Sadly however he refuses to come out into the open so I can safely escort him to the vets. My concern is now not only for Hercules, but for the stench now omitting from the kitchen. I am sure in time I will be able to open the adjoining door again and use copious levels of detergent to mask the smell. The now however, dinner parties are defiantly a no-no.

I must say I find your 'cat scan' 'joke' to be in poor taste. I am sure to an outsider this must seem humorous; however I have found the whole episode extremely distressing. I trust your pets never have to endure the trauma that has taken place recently in our household.

One 'positive' from your end is that your product does work, albeit it this conclusion has been arrived at by default.

P. Keriss

22. Blown tyre

From: Pat Keriss
To: Mates condoms
Subject: Faulty condoms

I am extremely concerned with regard to the ineptitude of your products and their not being 'fit for purpose'.

My son, Gerald, is now aged 18 and is about to become a father for the 3rd time (with three different females). Although a virile young man, he has been using your condoms every time for intercourse since he lost his virginity aged 16.

I purchase his condoms for him and have even demonstrated how he is to use the condoms for maximum effectiveness. Despite this, he has sired yet another child. The reason for this is down to the fact that your condoms do not work!

I would like an indication as to a way forward, be it with assistance toward (mounting) child maintenance costs, or other financial remuneration. I have always advocated mates above other brands such as Durex and I feel rather foolish having now seen that your products do not do what they say on the packet.

I look forward to a speedy resolution to this matter.

P. Keriss

From: Mates condoms
To: Pat Keriss
Subject: Faulty condoms

Dear Pat

Thank you for contacting with regard to Mates condoms. As you will be aware, our packaging states that the use of a condom cannot guarantee 100% protection against pregnancy. However, all of our condoms are manufactured to ISO 4074 :2002 Natural Latex Rubber Condoms –Requirements and Test Methods.

If you have any remaining condoms from the pack, or can advise me of the lot number found on the packaging and foils we can investigate this for you.

Pam Russell
Quality Assurance Manager

23. Barking

From: Pat Keriss
To: Kotex Tampons
Subject: Jason the dog

I have just been sickened to see the smiling woman on the home page of your website. This is contrary to my dreadful experiences using your product. An experience that I demand a swift response to...

My dog, Jason, is getting aged. With the onset of old age; he has suffered with an embarrassing problem which causes him to produce dihorrea at regular intervals. To cut a long (and messy) story short, I inserted one of your products into Jason's anus to soak up the excess faecal matter. This worked for a couple of days and I was pleased with the absorbency of your product. Although the pad was sodden when I took it out, it wasn't too messy (just a quick hand rinse in hot water seemed to get the majority off my hands). On the 3rd day, I could not find the tampon. I searched the flat over the next day and still couldn't find it.

The day after, Jason got very ill, and subsequently died a few hours later. I spoke to some friends at the pet cemetery and they claimed he could have suffered from toxic shock syndrome? Whether or not he did, I would like to know why your products are of such a poor design, that dogs have to die in order to satisfy your bottom line.

I am truly appalled and demand an explanation. Suffice to say, I won't be recommending your products to my friends/ other pet owners again.

P. Keriss

From: Kotex
To: Pat Keriss
Subject: Jason the dog

Dear Pat,

Thank you for contacting Kimberly-Clark. We are sorry to hear of your experience with your pet.
KOTEX® Tampons are Feminine Care products and for use only by women during menstruation. The product has been specifically designed for this use only and they have not been tested for any other use. In the instance described in your email, the product was not used for the intended purpose. In all matters relating to their health or that of their pets, we recommend consumers contact health professionals for advice - GPs or vets.

You can be confident that Kimberly-Clark is committed to providing safe, high-quality products for our consumers, as their well-being is of great importance to us as a responsible manufacturer. Extensive studies have been performed on each product to ensure its overall safety and performance for the intended purpose. Each component is evaluated to ensure that the material would not produce irritation.

Regarding Toxic Shock Syndrome, this is caused by the bacterium called Staphylococcus aureus, which exists normally in the nose, armpits, groin or vagina of about 1/3 of the healthy population. Sometimes strains of this bacterium give off a toxin that gets into the body, probably through the bloodstream. Although scientific data suggest that the use of tampons may increase the risk of TSS, tampons, themselves, have not been found to cause TSS.

We hope this information will be of help.

Yours sincerely,

Antonella Cassar
Consumer Services Department
Kimberly-Clark Europe

24. Mild green

From: Pat Keriss
To: Unilever (Fairy washing up liquid)
Subject: in a lather

I am a tad embarrassed to be writing to you, but I would like some urgent advice/ assistance.

As a normal, single, red blooded male, I sometimes feel the need to 'pleasure' myself. Last Tuesday, having returned home early from work, I was attempting to get aroused looking at adult pictures in a magazine. To be honest, it wasn't really happening although I felt very aroused.

I decided to use some Persil washing up liquid to aid my pleasure and, mixed with some water, I worked up a lather. I had a very pleasant experience using your product and satisfied myself within a few minutes.

About 30 minutes later however, I started to feel uncomfortable around the crotch region. I attempted to scratch it, but it caused a large area of redness and inflammation. Within an hour I was curled up naked in a ball in the hallway in absolute agony.

I ran a bath and managed to crawl in it and I scrubbed and scrubbed, again the inflammation got worse and I cried with the pain. I had to call my sister over. She arrived and saw the state of me curled on the floor, and the state of my genitalia. She was shocked and attempted to help by buying some calamine lotion. This also failed to help after application.

It is now not only sore, but the skin has cracked a little and is pussy and peeling. I am extremely concerned as I will be unable to go to work tomorrow. I am also too embarrassed to speak to the doctor. You must have experienced this before and I would appreciate any advice you can give me.
Also, I would appreciate it if you could put a clear warning on your packaging to stop other gentlemen from suffering from this agony.
P. Keriss
NO RESPONSE

25. The great indoors

From: Pat Keriss
To: Swift caravans
Subject: Tentavan

Hi,

I have an opportunity that I would like to pitch to you. I would like a speedy response as I have a number of other manufacturers who I would like to approach with my innovative new idea, but I thought I'd give you first refusal.

The idea is this.....the Tentavan.

Basically it is a caravan which has been cut in half (from top to bottom) leaving it 'dressed from the waist down' if you will. There is then a pull over top (like a convertible car) which goes over the van to produce a Tentavan....i.e. half caravan, half tent.

This has a number of benefits. On sunny days you can sit/ lay out in the sun in the confines/ comfort of your caravan. When it gets cold, pull over the tent section and its like glamping (camping in comfort). Children will enjoy the novelty of camping, but in the comfort of their own bed/ watching TV etc.

I have prototyped the product. There are a few design flaws which I am currently working on, such as the difficulty in towing the Tentavan above 40 mph (I am now designing an 'easy flow air system', to allow air to travel through the product whilst on the motorway), as well as the problem of lack of headspace when the tent section is erect.

I am sure you will be interested and would like to come and visit you at some stage over the next 2 weeks to do a deal.

I look forward to your reply.

P. Keriss

From: Swift Leisure
To: Pat Keriss
Subject: Tentavan

Dear Mr Keriss

Tentavan

Thankyou for your e mail.

I am very sorry but this is not a product we would be interested in at this time.

Thankyou for sharing your idea with us.

Yours Sincerely

Hayley Jones (Customer Service Advisor)

From: Pat Keriss
To: Swift Leisure
Subject: Tentavan

What a shame...and you haven't even seen my plans.

I have another idea....introducing.....the caraboat.

It is a caravan which is buoyed by a few welded on canoes, some ballast and a (I am thinking of a...) patent pending floatation device.

It allows the families to use their caravan whilst enjoying the sights and sounds of, for example, the Norfolk broads. It can be steered using paddles and the front door will be a 'horse box' style door, allowing family members to get in and out without getting wet.

Interested?

Pat Keriss

From: Swift Leisure
To: Pat Keriss
Subject: The caraboat

Dear Mr Keriss

**Thank you for your letter received with your idea of a caraboat, I'm sorry
but we have our own design team.**

Yours sincerely

From: Pat Keriss
To: Swift Leisure
Subject: The caraboat

Hi Lynne

Reading between the lines, I guess that is a veiled job offer?

I would be glad to jump aboard the design team should the overall package be right.

Around a 60k basic, final salary pension, 15% of the company net profits and BUPA cover for myself and my extended family would be a good starting point for negotiations I think.

As well as these ideas mentioned I am currently working on plans to deliver the 'caractor' to the agricultural market. It is a mix between a caravan and a tractor and, although in preliminary design stages, she signs are positive from the farming community thus far.

I look forward to our negotiations.

Pat

26. A common stamp

From: Pat Keriss
To: Tattoo club Great Britain
Subject: The Tramp Stamp Festival 2010

I have a proposition I would like to put to you in the expectation that the tcgb will get behind and backed my idea:

'The tramp stamp festival 2010'

The idea is to set up a music festival to rival the 'V' and Glastonbury festivals. It will be a weekend long celebration of tattoos and all they stand for. All acts will be tattooed (Robbie Williams/ Green day and others...) and acts will be presented onstage by certain aficionados of the stamp, such as David Beckham.

There will also be a Mr and Miss Nude Tramp Stamp competition 2010, with the winner receiving a free tattoo of any size anywhere on their body. This will show the beauty of the tattoo to non believers and can be used in the 2011 promotional material.

In addition to this, only punters who have tattoos will be allowed entry to the festival site. There will however be emergency tattooists on hand outside the venue to give tattoos to 'tramp stamp virgins' as my wife likes to call them.

Please let me know your initial thoughts.

P. Keriss

NO RESPONSE

27. Toy Story

From: Pat Keriss
To: Smyths toy store
Subject: WH?

I have just travelled back from a while overseas and I am disgusted with what has happened to one of my favourite stores.

When the hell did you drop the 'WH' from your name and stop selling stationary?

I went to a store the other day and it seemed to be predominantly toys in the store.

What the blazes is going on with your business?

P. Keriss

NO RESPONSE

28. To the wall

From: Pat Keriss
To: Woolworths
Subject: Stores?

I have been away overseas for a while and having got back last week I went to my local store. That was shut. I then went to the next nearest store. That was shut too.

What the bloody hell is going on??

P. Keriss

From: Woolworths
To: Pat Keriss
Subject: Stores?

Dear Customer

Thanks for your email.

We're sorry but we can't offer any advice of the previous Woolworths operation as
we've only bought the brand name. We have been advised to direct former customers and shareholders
to Deloittes, who are the administrators, via their email address at woolworthsplc@deloitte.co.uk. However
you could try their central London office on (0)20 7936 3000.
We hope this answers your question.

Kind Regards
Bilkish Bolton
Woolworths Customer Services Team

29. Long pot

From: Pat Keriss
To: Toys R'us
Subject: Pocket billiards

A friend of mine recently told me about a wonderful game called 'pocket billiards'. I have been unable to find this product anywhere.

Please can you tell me more about this product, how it is played and the cost? Also which stores stock it?

Many thanks

From: Toysrus
To: Pat Keriss
Subject: Pocket Billiards

Dear Mr Keriss,

Thank you for your recent e-mail.

We apologise that this item is not currently available on-line.

Please contact your local Toys R Us store, as this item may be available to purchase through them. You can locate your local store using our website guide, or by calling our freephone store locator on 0800 138 7777.

Should you have any further queries, please do not hesitate to contact us again.

Kind regards,

David Saveraux
Toys R Us Direct

From: Pat Keriss
To: Toysrus
Subject: Snooker

Dear David,

Will do. And thankyou.

There is another game I am searching for....do you stock a branded product 'Jen Ital' snooker?

Many thanks

P. Keriss

From: Toysrus
To: Pat Keriss
Subject: Snooker

Dear Mr Keriss,

Thank you for your recent e-mail.

Toys R Us Direct do not currently stock 'Jen Ital' snooker and apologise if this causes you any disappointment. Toys R Us Direct add products to the site on a regular basis improving and adding to our range available.

Please contact your local store who will be able to tell you if the item is available to buy through the store.

If the item is available, they will be able to provide details of the range available and the price. You can locate your local store by using our on-line store guide, or by calling our freephone store locator on 0800 038 8889.

We hope this is of help to you. Should you require any further assistance, then please do not hesitate to contact us again.

Kind regards,
Rachel Brown
Toys R Us Direct

From Pat Keriss
To: Toysrus
Subject: Tug
It's a shame you do not have Jen Ital snooker in stock.

Do you instead stock 'Tug'? This is part of the P. Narse stable of products.

Pat Keriss

From: Toysrus
To: Pat Keriss
Subject: Tug

Dear Mr. Keriss,

Thank you for your recent e-mail.

We apologise that this item is not currently available on-line.

Please contact your local Toys R Us store, as this item may be available to purchase through them. You can locate your local store using our website guide, or by calling our freephone store locator on 0800 138 7777.

Should you have any further queries, please do not hesitate to contact us again.

Kind regards,

Oliver Watters
Toys R Us Direct

30. Candle vandal

From: Pat Keriss
To: Harrods
Subject: Huwax

I have a wonderful product I would like you to stock. It is called the 'Huwax'. It is basically a labour of love candle which has taken nearly a decade to produce and will sell at a premium.

It is made from my own human ear wax which I have saved, pressed and tested. It lights and acts as a candle and has been described as 'unique', 'original' and 'magnificent' by my acquaintances.

Please let me know when you would like me to come and give you a demonstration of the product.

P. Keriss

NO RESPONSE

31. TV times

From: P.Keriss
To: CBeebies (BBC)
Subject: Swinging implication

I am extremely concerned about the double entendres used in the programme 'something special' on CBeebies.

The main character Justin invites Mr Tumble on to the show. Obviously a 'tumble' is a double entendre for a sexual encounter. He also talks about his 'special friend'. This would imply a 'friend with benefits' or 'f**k buddy'.

Please can you explain?

From: BBC
To: Pat Keriss
Subject: Swinging implication

Dear Mr Keriss
Thanks for your e-mail regarding 'Something Special'. I understand that you're concerned with what you believe to be double entendres in this series.
These programmes are aimed at very young children with language development difficulties, and exploring, with the help of Macaton signing, everyday situations such as going shopping and preparing for bed. I can assure you there's no hidden sexual meaning behind anything contained in this series. I realise you may continue to have concerns with this programme. Therefore, let me assure you I've registered your comments on our audience log. This is a daily report of audience feedback that's circulated to many BBC staff, including members of the BBC Executive Board, channel controllers and other senior managers.
The audience logs are seen as important documents that can help shape decisions about future programming and content.
All feedback we receive, whether positive or negative is always appreciated. Thanks again for taking the time to contact us with your views.
Stefan Curran, BBC Complaints

32. Cleaning up

From: Pat Keriss
To: Vax
Subject: Vaxman

I have written a new jingle for your advertising campaigns. I have enclosed the lyrics which I am willing to licence out. Please contact me when you have read them. I am sure you will agree they are original and that they will increase your sales figures, even after a few plays by at least 5 fold:

Vaxman.

I'll tell you how it will be. Vaxman!
Dust for you, no dust for me. Vaxman!
Cos I'm the Vaxman. Yeah, the Vaxma'a'a'a'n.

Should your home appear too small,
Be thankful I will vax it all.
'Cause I'm the vaxman,
Yeah, I'm the vaxman.

If you drive a car, I'll vax the seat
If you drop dinner, Ill vax your meat
If you home grows mould, Ill vax with heat
If you take a walk, I'll vax your feet.

vaxman!
Cause I'm the vaxman,
Yeah, I'm the vaxman.

Don't ask me what I do it for,
If you want me to, ill vax some more.
Cause I'm the vaxman,
Yeah, I'm the vaxman.

Now my advice for those who die, (vaxman)
Declare your cleanliness when you reach the sky, Cause I'm the vaxman,
Yeah, I'm the vaxman.

NO RESPONSE

33. Hanna Barbera

From: Pat Keriss
To: The FA
Subject: WAG: The cartoon

I have devised a fantastic cartoon based around 'birds'. The idea is simple, I draw the pictures and come up with storylines and the FA sanction my use of their players names and logo.

Cartoon 1: The WAGS v the celebs.

The players will all be based around bird names. The line ups are the following:

WAGS:
Peter Grouse, Bobby Moorehen, Paul Finch, Ostrichard Wright, Kez Brown, Wrenold Koeman, Crane Rooney, Robert Greenfinch, Emunuel Adabayor, JayJay Okocha

The celebs:
Chicky Butcher, Michael Larkinson, Gannet Street Porter, Simon C-Owl, Bobby Kingfisher, Arthur Mallard, Eddie Buzzard, Dickie Bird, Alan Partridge, Alistair Starling, Thrush Abbott.

Please let me know your thoughts and when it will suitable for me to come and meet you regarding this venture.

P.Keriss

NO RESPONSE

34. A load of old pony

From: Pat Keriss
To: Pony world magazine
Subject: Geraldine

With great sadness, my pony, Geraldine, has become very ill and has little time left.

With this in mind, I would like some advice.....

Having lost my job a while ago, finances are tight. I have decided to have Geraldine put down and would like to know if you have any contacts of ethical suppliers/ purchasers of quality horse/ pony meat. I'm thinking 'France', although shipping of the carcass may prove costly.

Do you have any contacts who may be interested in purchasing kg's of quality pony meat at reasonable prices?

I am quite happy to sell her on as 'horse meat' as I believe the horsemeat market is not frowned upon in relation to pony meat which is (according to my friend) quite gristly.

Your thoughts/ advice are greatly appreciated.

Many thanks

P. Keriss

NO RESPONSE

35. Mans best friend

From: Pat Keriss
To: Dogs monthly magazine
Subject: Bonding

As an experienced dog owner, I would like to pass some advice to other owners who wish to bond with puppies.

When my bitch Emma had puppies, I decided to become fully involved from the moment of birth. For some reason, when I saw Emma licking her puppies clean after delivery, I knelt on the floor and assisted her in licking the puppies clean. Although a strange taste (sickly, yet sweet), Emma didn't seem to mind. Her puppies in turn immediately bonded with us both to leave them with 2 mummies!

I have had bitches give birth and not used this method and have not become as close to any of the puppies. All of the puppies I have licked after being born have bonded and welcomed me as a maternal figure. I would fully recommend it as a method for anyone to use to bond completely with their little darlings.

I would suggest a little gargle of mouthwash after, although the taste becomes quite comforting after a few attempts.

P.Keriss

NO RESPONSE

36. A sticky situation

From: Pat Keriss
To: The Erotic Review
Subject: Sticky Butcher

Hi,
I am an avid reader of Erotic text and prose and would like to submit a series of stories revolving around a hero I have devised and copyrighted, a former soap actor called 'Sticky Butcher'. I would like to offer my services as a regular columnist with a different story/ case being solved by 'Sticky' every week.

The idea is simple. Sticky has a special power. His cum/ semen/ babyfat is made of (PVA strength) glue. This was caused by a genetic defect as a child, similar to the genetic make up of Superman, but different. Every episode he solves community, and national problems using his power to alleviate sticky situations.

Episode 1: Sticky travels to Wales. As he drives over the Severn Bridge, he notices it is shaking and that the bridge is falling apart at the crucial joins that holds such structures in place. With the Welsh running from their cars screaming 'ffwcio' (Welsh for 'fuck!'). He leaps into action. He carefully manoeuvres himself in the press up position and leans over a large gap forming on the road. He undoes his fly and releases his impressive phallus and masturbates furiously. With seconds to spare he ejaculates and his PVA cum shoots between the gap and engulfs the danger area, thus holding the bridge together, giving the welsh time to escape and the bridge engineers a crucial window in which to save the bridge.

There are plenty of other scrapes Sticky can get into and I thought I could also introduce some other superpower sexual celebrity friends such as 'Wank Lamphard', 'Pricky Gervais' and 'Martin Bell-end'. I am sure this is the kind of original prose you are seeking. Please let me know I am OK to proceed with my initial story for your next edition...

P. Keriss
NO RESPONSE

37. Plastic tragitastic

From Pat Keriss:
To: M&S
Subject: Product quality

I am writing to complain bitterly about your cost cutting across the store, but particularly with regard to your carrier bags.

Having lost my job 7 months ago, I sadly cannot afford to shop in M&S too frequently. However, when I do shop there I always ensure I obtain at least a dozen carrier bags.

To save money, I sometimes use the carrier bags as a barrier method. I have saved alot of money using this method and it acts as a powerful birth control aid.

Last Friday however, when my wife was at her most fertile, the bag split at the point of no return. We are now in a state of panic that because your bags are shoddily made now, we could be expecting a child, One for which we are neither mentally or financially prepared.

To say I'm disappointed in the lax standards in your products now would be an understatement.

P. Keriss

From: Marks and Spencer
To: Pat Keriss
Subject: Product Quality

Dear Pat Keriss,

Thank you for you email.
I am sorry that you were disappointed wIth the quality of our carrier bags. Please be assured that I have fully logged your comments on our systems. This will alert our teams that oversee our carriers to your concerns. Thank you again for getting in touch.
Kind regards,
George Mason, Customer Advisor
Customer Services Team

38. Downsizing

From: Pat Keriss
To: Slimming world
Subject: weight loss

Hello,

I would like to offer you my help as a way of thanking you for my dramatic weight loss.

I used to weight 30 stone. I now weigh 12. This is due to your wonderful programme.

I decided to diet the day I went for a trek on my beloved pony, Tessa. I had been riding Tess for a short while when I heard a sickening crack as Tessa lurched forward.

To cut a long story short, I had broken Tess' spine through my weight sitting on her back. Against medical advice I decided not to put Tessa down and she still lives today.

Although she cannot walk, I arrange physio for her daily and we manage to wheel her about in a specialist equine product, a 'ponychair'.

I would like to offer to come and talk to your groups regarding my weight loss as well as giving them the chance to meet Tessa who can be wheeled into the meetings as a warning to other overweight pony lovers.

Please let me know when you would like us to come and give the first talk?

Regards,

P. Keriss

NO RESPONSE

39. Crowning glory

From: Pat Keriss
To: Venezuelan Embassy
Subject: Congratulations!

I read the headline 'Venezuela wins 6th Miss Universe crown' with joy in my heart! Congratulations!
Your historic 6th victory certainly gets Venezuela on the map, which is to be commended!

My only concern is your country getting the reputation as being full to the rafters with gorgeous, vivacious, sexy, scat clad, sultry, pecker dance inducing, lithe, fit, stunning, puppy dog eyed hunnies.

I myself have visited Venezuela and although there are couple of tasty birds dotted about, I saw truckloads of right old mingers.

In 4 weeks backpacking, I had intercourse with around 18 of your country women. Lovely girls one and all personality wise. They did your country proud........but in the sack they were shocking. When they smiled, I got the words 'canine' 'licking' 'yellow' 'peril' 'off'' 'stinging' and 'nettle' ingrained in my head.

I am just concerned you don't give out the wrong impressions of the venezwemen.

P. Keriss

NO RESPONSE

40. Causing a stink

From: Pat Keriss
To: Top Trumps
Subject: Top trumps

I have invented a new 'top trump' that I would like to go into Business with you to use. It is called 'Top trumps top trumps'!

Basically a 'trump 'is a fart. So why not have a pack of your cards featuring bottoms with attributes such as 'Velocity', 'stink factor', 'smelliness', 'skidability' and 'dampness'.

I have taken a number of pictures of my friend's bums and am busy building up a set of cards.

Please tell me when you would like to meet regarding my proposal?

Thanks

NO RESPONSE

41. Spoken

From: Pat Keriss
To: Cannondale Cycles
Subject: Menstruation cycle

I have an idea for a bicycle that I would like to go into partnership with your company.

It is aimed at females and is called the 'menstruation cycle'.

Basically it will be themed around the female time of the month and will be coloured blood red. The seat will be in the shape of a sanitary towel and there will be bits of string woven around the spokes on the wheel.

I believe this would be a huge success in the UK and would offer comfort all month around, not just for one week a month.

The slogan could be 'Buy a menstruation cycle. It's that time of the month. Period!'

I look forward to your response.

P. Keriss

NO RESPONSE

42. Glue

To: Bostik
From: Pat Keriss
Subject: Man glue

I have devised a new product that I believe you will be interested in licensing from me.

It is a novelty glue item shaped like an erect phallus.

I call this item the 'Man Goo Gluestik'.

Basically upon pressing the tip of the phallus onto a surface it emits white glue. This will be a great novelty item and also will keep up the morale of the building industry in these troubling times.

Upon your response I would be pleased to offer you a demonstration of my man goo glue.

Regards

P. Keriss

NO RESPONSE

43. Shapely soaker

From: Pat Keriss
To: Tena
Subject: Chinese Tena

Hi,

I have had a great idea for a product extension aimed solely at the Chinese market.

Why not aim a square shaped bladder weakness product at Chinese men.

Introducing 'Tena Men square'.

This is a clever play on words I'm sure you'll agree and it will go down a storm in china where 1 in every 4 men has (according to my research) either soiled themselves or suffered from an excess of man dribble.

I look forward to your response.

P. Keriss

From: Tena
To: Pat Keriss
Subject: Chinese Tena

Dear P Keriss

Thank you for your email.

There are no immediate plans for such a product as our TENA For Men pads are designed to give extra protection for all men. I have passed your comments on to the Product Development Team who monitor consumer feedback very closely. It is only through regular feedback that we can understand our customers' needs better.

We appreciate you taking the time to contact us.

Kind Regards, Claire

44. Wodka hell?

From: Pat Keriss
To: Absolute Radio
Subject: Vodka

I bought a couple of lovely bottles of your vodka in Russia last year but cannot find any stockists here in the UK.

It is a refined tipple flavoured aniseed and cherry.

Can you tell me how much 5 bottles would be?

Cheers

Pat Keriss

NO RESPONSE

45. Sonnet

From: Pat Keriss
To: British Shakespeare Society
Subject: Writing

Hi,

I would like to write content for your website/ publications.

I fucking love shakespeare. He is the nuts. From his shit hot sonnets to his fucking awesome plays...he is one bad motherfucker.

I write for loads of publications and know how to write sensitive prose whilst sticking to every cunting deadline set.

I wont fucking let you down.

Please let me know what you can offer me and I can show you the size of my bollocks (literary speaking of course).

Keep your shit tight.

P. Keriss

NO RESPONSE

46. It's a fair cop

From: Pat Keriss
To: Liverpool FC
Subject: The Dirk Kite

I have recently manufactured and sold a large number of the 'Dirk Kite'. This is basically a kite with Dirk's likeness on it.

I would now like written permission that you will also allow me to use the Liverpool crest on the kite reverse.

Many thanks

P.Keriss

**From: Liverpool FC
To: Pat Keriss
Subject: Dirk Kite**

Pat,

Thank you for your email.

Unfortunately we will not be able to grant you permission to use our club crest on your product as the Liverpool FC crest is a registered trademark, therefore it can only be used by Official LFC partners.

As you are not an Official partner of the clubs, including the Liverpool FC crest on your product would infringe on our trademark.

**Kind Regards
Licensing**

From: Pat Keriss
To: Liverpool FC
Subject: Dirk Kite

Dear Susan,

Fair enough. At least I can still use the Dirkhead on the kite I suppose.

I have produced another product which I am hoping you may want to sell in your club shop? It's a T Shirt with a semi clad Martin Skrtel wearing a skirt. Underneath it says, 'I wear a skirt well. I'm Martin Skrtel'. They have gone down a storm at boot sales thus far.

Cheers

Pat

47. Sheathing environmentalists

From: Pat Keriss
To: Hertsmere council
Subject: refused refuse

I am a keen advocate of recycling in the Hertsmere area.

To this end, I have saved all of my condoms/ sheaths over the last few years in order to save the planet (and unwanted pregnancy!).

I spoke to the domestic waste engineer last week and he refuse(d) to take them.

I have around 7 kilos of washed out used sheaths and was wondering who to send them to for recycling?

Regards

P.Keriss

From: Hertsmere Council
To: Pat Keriss
Subject: Refused refuse

Dear Mr Keriss
Thank you for your email.
Your enquiry has been forwarded to our Waste Management Team for their response.

Please note should you wish to contact them direct, their email address is street.scene@hertsmere.gov.uk**.**

Yours sincerely
Customer Services

From: Hertsmere Council
To: Pat Keriss
Subject: Refused refuse

Dear Resident,
Thank you for your email.
Unfortunately, we do not deal with recycling of this type of material. I would suggest visiting the wasteaware website www.wasteaware.org.uk or contacting them on 08457 425 000. They will be able to offer advice on where (and if) your condoms can be recycled.
Kind Regards
Jade Reynolds
Street Scene Services, Hertsmere Borough Council

48. Norway is that a new car

From: Pat Keriss
To: Ford UK
Subject: Fjord

Recently on a trip to Norway I purchased a second hand Fjord Siesta.

Upon returning to the UK, and my car breaking down, I have been informed that this car is not a Norwegian version of your car, but is in fact a replica being widely sold throughout Norway.

I need a clutch bearing for this vehicle and I am hoping you can help?

P. Keriss

NO RESPONSE

49. Toffee crumble

From: Pat Keriss
To: Everton FC
Subject: Pienaars

I have recently produced (and sold) a large number of T Shirts with a picture of a phallus and the likeness of Steven Pienaar in the phallus head.

Underneath are the words 'There's nothing like a true blue Pienaars!', which, I am sure you'll agree is a clever play on words.

I am producing a further range of SP goods for sale and was hoping you would agree to my adding the Everton logo/ crest onto the tops?

Up the Toffee's!

P. Keriss

From: Everton FC
To: Pat Keriss
Subject: Pienaars

Pat

I have no intention of supplying you with any logos or permissions for this type of product.

I don't expect you have received written permission from Steven's representatives for use of his image? Can you supply an image of the t-shirt and other merchandise as I will pass it to our IP team who will be in touch to take action against you for unauthorised use of player and club imagery.

You will need to take this off sale and destroy all product made to date. We absolutely do not want players portrayed in this way.
Regards
Gary Wilton

From: Pat Keriss
To: Everton FC
Subject: Pienaars

Dear Gary,

Very amusing! As if you have image rights whatever they are?

So can I use the logo or not?

I also have ideas for other Everton based products including a T shirt with Joseph Yobo's face on saying 'I'm not just a Yobbo!'. I also have a T shirt about to be printed with ABBA singing the words 'Knowing me, knowing Lou-is Saha...'.

I would be interested in your thoughts.

Cheers

Pat

50. A balls up

From: Pat Keriss
To: Ed Balls MP
Subject: T Shirts

Hi,

I am a long time Labourite and fundraiser for the cause.

I have recently had 5000 t shirts printed which I am about to distribute and I was wondering if you'd like me to send you a few to wear when campaigning next year?

They contain a picture of you with the words: 'The Tories may have bollo**s, but we've got Balls!'.

Let me know how many you'd like and I'll drop them in the post.

Keep up the good work!

P. Keriss

NO RESPONSE

51. Fragrant vagrant

From: Pat Keriss
To: Tramp (lifestyle) magazine
Subject: Trevor

Hi,

I have befriended a tramp called Trevor who lives underneath the Leytonstone railway arches. I have a few pictures and wondered if you'd like to run a story on him in your next edition?

He has an interesting back story having been a crack cocaine addict and former armed robber. Lovely guy besides that though so he is.

P. Keriss

NO RESPONSE

52. Free the meat

From: Pat Keriss
To: Pukka Pies
Subject: Meat

I have been a purveyor of Pukka pies for many years. As a vegetarian, I love the fact that they don't contain any real meat and I can enjoy them by the barrowload.

On Saturday however I was shocked to discover what seemed to be a lump of meat in one of your pies. Is this now standard procedure to offer up a product with real meat in?

Pat Keriss

From: Pukka Pies
To: Pat Keriss
Subject: Meat

Dear Mrs Keriss

Thank you for your email. Please could you let me know which products you purchase and use by dates if you have them. Also could I have your postal address.

I am a little confused by your email as we only sell two vegetarian products.

Yours sincerely

Ms Kerry Dickens
Customer Services Manager

From: Pat Keriss
To: Pukka Pies
Subject: Meat

Dear Mr Dickens,

Firstly I am Mr, not a Mrs!

As stated I have eaten Pukka Pies for a number of years and have never encountered any 'real' meat until recently, just the processed meat substitute that is passed off as meat. This for me is not a problem as a) I enjoy it, and b) it doesn't play havoc with my constitution. For example I inadvertently eat a 'Ginsters' Pie recently and that had real meat in it which left me (in the words of the late great Johnny Cash) with a 'ring of fire'.

When did you replace the meat substitute with real meat? Can you not change back?

Also, I am sure you have sold more than 2 vegetarian products!

Many thanks

MR Pat Keriss

From: Pukka Pies
To: Pat Keriss
Subject: Meat

Dear Mr Keriss

Thank you for your email and I am sorry that I confused your gender.

We have always used the same cuts of meat from the forequarter of bullock beef, we have never used "processed" meat. We have our own butchery and the cuts of meat are either brisket or chuck rolls, we have not changed this process for 47 years. We dice or mince the meat in our butchery so we have complete control of the meat quality.

Thank you for your interest in our company.

Yours sincerely.
Mr Kerry Dickens,
Customer Services Manager

From: Pat Keriss
To: Pukka Pies
Subject: Meat

Dear Mr Dickens,

It doesn't taste like real meat, like Bernard Matthews does for example. Maybe it's time to change a 47 year old process? I just trust the machinery used to butcher the poor loves has been cleaned and maintained thoroughly in that time.

Pat Keriss

53. A little bit of jazz

From: Pat Keriss
To: Razzle porn magazine
Subject: Ethel

I love the magazine! My girlfriend also loves the magazine...its great! I have always been into older women. I am 36; my current girlfriend is 88 and is rather ill. It has been her wish since we have been in a relationship to pose for a pornographic magazine. Would it be possible to arrange a shoot and publish the pictures? Although overweight (size 26), she has a lovely figure with not too much excess skin. We can pose her in a way so that the colostomy bag is not in view.

She would not expect payment for the shoot (she has 'mild' Alzheimer's so will forget the shoot within a few hours anyway). If however you want to bung me a few quid for expenses, that would be great. I am willing to let her hang around after the shoot should you wish to picture her with any objects/ people/ possibly small rodent type animals too.

I look forward to your response.

Pat Keriss

NO RESPONSE

54. Cock of the century

From: Pat Keriss
To: Tim Westwood
Subject: Homonatural

Hi AJ,

I am a huge Westwood fan and would like to enquire about booking him for an event I am running next summer.

It is called 'Homonatural 2010'. Basically it is a gay naturist festival in Somerset. I expect around 10000 people to attend and we will be having the best in 'gay music' including (to be confirmed) marc almond, right said fred and the pet shop boys.

My hope is that Westwood will agree to compere the weekend?

Although nudity is mandatory, if he is uneasy about going nude, then would he be prepared to present in a thong in order to appease the paying punters?

There will be free backstage massages for VIP's as well as a full rider.

The masseurs are very good and will of course provide any extras Westwood requires (discreetly) at no extra cost.

Please let me know his availability and approximate cost.

Westside!

Pat Keriss

NO RESPONSE

55. Its going to be huge

To: Rik Wallers management
From: Pat Keriss
Subject: Rik Waller

Hi

I am a huge Rik Waller fan. I also happen to run an adult entertainment company. I have a proposition for Rik...

I am making a film about BBW (Big beautiful women) and I would like Rik to star. Basically this would involve full penetration (some back door action too) with some (clean) young fillies. Rik would of course be paid handsomely and would have a full rider for food and drink.

The filming should take a whole day and there will be young 'helping hands' available to get Rik in the party mood!

Please let me know if Rik would be up for this and his daily rate.

Also, we may wish to shoot a scene which involves a little 'teabagging'. Would Rik be adverse to this? If not, would he rather teabag, or be teabagged?

Regards

**Pat Keriss
From: Ron Martin Management
To: Pat Keriss
Subject: Rik Waller**

Hi Pat

Could You give mr Martin a ring please on XXXX XXXXXX

Kind regards

**Lucy
Ron Martin Management**

From: Pat Keriss
To: Ron Martin management
Subject: Rik Waller

Hi Lucy

I'm currently filming a popporn spectacular in Spain based on a mythical tale where Boyzone's Stephen Gately falls in lust with the 'Backstreet Boys' (with painful consequences for the Gately!).

Luckily for Gately, Ronan saves the day (expertly played by Martin 'the meat' McDonnell.

I will call on my return. In principle, is Rik up for this if the money is right?

Regards

56. A close shave

From: Pat Keriss
To: Groom and Go
Subject: Grooming

Hi Michelle

A friend gave me your contact details.

How much would you charge to groom my 16 year old bitch?

Pat Keriss

From: Groom and Go
To: Pat Keriss
Subject: Grooming

Hi Pat,

Sorry but you haven't told me what type or size of dog she is.

Small dogs basic wash and brush is £20 and full groom is £25
Medium dogs basic is £25 to £30 full groom
Large dogs basic is £30 to £35 full groom

the full groom includes any trimming, clipping and nails.

I hope this helps.

(the bath is a walk in bath so would be easier for an elderly dog.)

Kind regards
Michelle

From: Pat Keriss
To: Groom and Go
Subject: Grooming

Hi Michelle

She is St Bernard called Bernie (short for Bernadette after a former lover).

I would class her as humungous, so large should suffice.

Do you have experience of grooming large teenage bitches of this age? Or do you usually work with younger?

Regards

Pat

From: Groom and Go
To: Pat Keriss
Subject: Grooming

Hi Pat,

I do have a regular Pyrenean mountain dog of 10 - she suffers alopecia from stress of losing her sister. You must be doing something right to get such a large dog to that age!

I'm sure we will manage. Is she able to stand for longish periods of time or would she attempt to sit down? Either way it's not a problem. Probably best to give you an afternoon appointment of around 3ish so we can take our time...

I could do Tues or Thursday next week if this suits you. please let me know and let me have your address and phone number.

many thanks
Michelle

From: Pat Keriss
To: Groom and Go
Subject: Grooming

That's great! I love mounting dogs. Shame about her sister....how did she depart? Such a shame.

I feed her on the finest cuts of meat and pamper her basically. She wants for very little. I love her dearly.

She too had a rough time with a previous owner who didn't treat her as the lady she is. He was a little too affectionate by all counts if you catch my drift. She has a slight limp which I am sure is linked to her mistreatment.

She is better sitting. I should warn you she does have problem controlling her bowels especially when sitting on porcelain. Is your bath plastic or porcelain? She doesn't tend to pass motions as often on plastic strange as that sounds.

Next thurs may be good....2ish perhaps?

Pat

From:Groom and Go
To: Pat Keriss
Subject: Grooming

Hi Pat,

Thurs pm is good but not sure if I can make it for 2 as I've got 2 others to do in Borehamwood first. I would be there asap once Ive finished those - (one of them is an overweight cocker spaniel who gets stressed out so she takes a while to do.)

can you give me your address and telephone number please so I know where I'm coming to and so I can contact you if running late. (The mountain dogs sister died suddenly of a tumour on her spine I think). I look forward to meeting you and Bernie on Thurs 1st Oct.
regards
Michelle

57. Meow

From: Pat Keriss
To: Sally (Sallywags cat grooming)
Subject: trim

Hi Sally,

I have a pussy I affectionately call 'Nooni'.

She hasn't had a touch up for a long time. If I bring her to your premises, how much would you charge to trim my pussy?

Many thanks

Pat Keriss

From: Sallywags
To: Pat Keriss
Subject: Trim

Hi Pat,

Apologies for the delay, I charge £50 for cats.
Look forward to hearing from you.

Thanks Sally

From: Pat Keriss
To: Sallywags
Subject: trim

Hi Sally,

That's terrific. At the same time is it possible to give my other cat (a kitten called quim) a trim?

Regards

Pat

58. Cheesemonger

From: Pat Keriss
To: Peter Shilton management
Subject: Peter Stilton

I am president of the UK cheese federation.

This year we are celebrating Stilton and we were hoping to hire Peter to come and give a talk about his career (and add some humorous cheese related stories) if possible?

We would market the event as 'an evening with Peter Stilton' which is a clever play on words.

Please can you let me know if Peter would be available for such an event?

Many thanks

Pat Keriss

From: Peter Shilton management
To: Pat Keriss
Subject: Peter Stilton

Good Morning Pat,

Thank you for your enquiry from Peter's page, it was really great to
hear from you.

The below is something that Peter would most certainly be interested in.
If you could please come back to me with a date and I can then check
this in his diary and send you his fee.

I shall really look forward to hearing from you

Kindest Regards
Lucy

From: Pat Keriss
To: Lucy (Peter Shilton management)
Subject: Peter Stilton

Hi Lucy,

I'm looking at maybe some date in November? What day is best for Peter? Maybe the 25th?

We will also provide a nice selection of cheeses for Peter's rider as well as a number to take home.

Would he be averse to wearing a specially made 'cheesestraw' hat for publicity shots?

I look forward to your response.

Many thanks

Pat

From: Lucy (Peter Shilton management)
To: Pat Keriss
Subject: Peter Stilton

Hi Pat,

Please can you let me know the fee that you have to offer to Peter and I can approach him with this?

However I know Peter would be happy with you calling the evening 'an evening with Peter Stilton' I'm afraid.

Look forward to hearing from you

Kind Regards

Lucy

From: Pat Keriss
To: Lucy (Peter Shilton management)
Subject: Peter Stilton

That's great that he is agreeable to 'an evening with Peter Stilton'...thanks for arranging that Lucy.

What's the going rate? I'm thinking around £5000 cheque or £4500 cash or £4300 cash including our top of the range cheese rider.

Please let me know your thoughts.

Regards

Pat

ps. Is he OK to wear the cheesstraw hat for publicity shots?

From: Lucy (Peter Shilton management)
To: Pat Keriss
Subject: Peter Stilton

Hi Pat,

It is probably best that you give me a call to discuss in more detail and then I can take all the information to Peter to discuss with him.

I miss typed my email, I am afraid that Peter will not be happy with the evening being called 'an evening with Peter Stilton'

Look forward to discussing this with you further

Kindest Regards

Lucy

From: Pat Keriss
To: Lucy (Peter Shilton management)
Date: Tuesday 6th October 2009
Subject: Peter Stilton

That's a shame, I really thought he was up for it...his name has certainly been the 'cheese knees' in the office recently.

Sadly (for Peter) we can only use him if the evening is with Peter 'Stilton'. We have another couple of possibles anyhow including Eastenders Adam Woodyat who has agreed to 'an evening with Edam Woodyat', and we are in discussions with the management of the woman who plays 'Brie' in desperate housewives, although her cheese rider is outrageous to be frank.

Another possibility is 'an evening with Wensleydale Winton' although we are unsure as to whether our members would be agreeable to a homosexual discussing his cheese.

Thanks anyway

Pat

59. Feeling ruff

From: Pat Keriss
To: Love Honey sex toys
Subject: canine mishap

I require some urgent advice. Whilst playing with my dog on the bed the other day, my rabbit (which had been applied with lubrication and was ready for use by me later on in the evening) somehow became inserted into my dog's anus. The force in which it entered has caused some kind of rupture and he has not stopped bleeding (a steady trickle) for the last 48 hours.

Do you have any suggestions? What have you advised when this has happened with previous customers?

The poor love won't let me go near him. As well as blood, he is becoming matted with faeces and is also sticky with jam which was another unfortunate by product of the other evening's mishap.

Pat Keriss

NO RESPONSE

60. Chin chin

From: Pat Keriss
To: Hair scientists
Subject: Beard

I am a 36 year old female. About 6 months ago after a volatile (same sex) union, I split with my partner. A few days after I noticed a growth of hair on my chin. The hair is now around 5 inches long and is what can only be described as a 'goatee'. Further to that the hair is not normal. It is wiry and very similar to pubic hair. The mess in the bed after I scratch it during the night is similar to the debris left after a coital session.

I have not left the house in weeks and my only contact is with a gentleman friend who has a fetish for what he calls 'bearded ladies'.

If I'm honest I have grown to enjoy the feeling somewhat, but socially it has left me in a pickle.

I would appreciate any advice.

Pat Keriss

From: The tricological society
To: Pat Keriss
Subject: Beard

Dear Ms Keriss

Thank you for your enquiry.

The symptoms you describe suggest an endocrine response. I suggest you refer to your GP with a possible request for dermatology / endocrinology.

Best wishes

Barry J Stevens FTTS
Registrar

61. Well travelled

From: Pat Keriss
To: Gipsy tights
Subject: Tight spot

Under legislation you really should change your name to Traveller tights.

The term 'Gipsy' is associated with racist overtones and should not be used to advertise wares.

Another possibility is 'pikey tights' which has a certain ring to it.

Have you verified your position with the campaign for racial equality?

Pat Keriss

NO RESPONSE

62. Pride of the north

From: Pat Keriss
To: North Lincs council
Subject: Scunthorpe

Dear Simon,

I am arranging a pan European festival for rude place name in 2010.

So far we have the following confirmed participants: Bell End (Worcestershire), Bollock (Philippines), Crotch Lake (Canada), Clit (Romania), Dickshit (India), Fanny Burn (Scotland), Fucking (Austria), Labia (Belgium), Minge (Lithuania), Semen (Bulgaria), Vagina (Russia) and Wankie (Zimbabwe).

Our sponsors (who have a terrific sense of humour (a famous brewers) are arranging for a long, all expenses paid weekend at (probably) the La Manga resort in Spain.

We are a bit short on the English contingent and wondered if you be interested in representing Scunthorpe at the event? It seems to be the only town with a cu*t in it to be frank.

I would appreciate a quick response as dates need to be finalised and the resort booked.

Regards

Pat Keriss

NO RESPONSE

63. Feck that

From: Pat Keriss
To: Austrian tourist board
Subject: Place name

Hello

I am currently assigned to writing an article about your place name in Tarsdorf called 'Fucking'. I have been asked to produce an article on the effect on tourism the place name has.

I would appreciate you attempting to answer some of the following questions for me:

Does fucking embrace tourists?
Is fucking a romantic place for a weekend?
Do fucking families resent the visitors to their town?
What fucking landmarks are there?
Is fucking good for the elderly people?
Do visitors abuse fucking and all it has to offer?
Do courting couples enjoy fucking?

If you could give me a brief summary of all my fucking enquiries I would appreciate it prior to my fucking visit.

Regards

Pat Keriss

From: Austrian tourist board
To: Pat Keriss
Subject: Fucking

Dear Mr. Keriss,

Thank you for your email. In this case we kindly ask you to get in contact with the local tourist board
I am sure our colleagues can help you further and I guess it would not be the first inquiring on the place "Fucking" from England. I hope to have been of help.
Best regards, Ursula Schiller

64. Glamping

From: Pat Keriss
To: Gelert (camping company)
Subject: Lynx 300

I recently purchased a Lynx 300 sleeping bag. I decided to take a trip to Snowdonia where, I must admit I wasn't amply prepared wearing only a t shirt, flip flops and shorts. Unexpectedly, the weather turned bad so I pitched my tent and got wrapped up in the Lynx 300.

A few hours later the weather cleared somewhat. I attempted to get out of the bag but found myself stuck completely. No matter how hard I tried I couldn't undo the fastener and my arms were stuck (one by my side, one around my groin area). I ended up like this for 14 hours until I was rescued by a passing hiking party. This proved extremely embarrassing as I had defecated and urinated in the bag (I had no choice).

I now demand a full refund and compensation for embarrassment caused not only for the hiking party seeing me this way, but by other climbers/ hikers seeing me in the sodden state as I walked back to my car.

Pat Keriss

From: Gelert.com
To: Pat Keriss
Subject: Lynx 300

Dear Customer,

I have received your following email regarding your Lynx 300

Gelert Ltd is a wholesale company and does not therefore have a contract directly with customers.

If you have any problems you would need to discuss these with the retailer you purchased the item from.
Kim Farrant
Customer Service Administrator, Gelert ltd

From: Pat Keriss
To: Gelert.com
Subject: Lynx 300

Dear Kim

It is that kind of 'dear customer' fob off e mail that gives company like yours short thrift.

The issue is the quality of the products you sell as wholesale.

Take your responsibility like a man!

Pat Keriss

From: Gelert.com
To: Pat Keriss
Subject: Lynx 300

Dear Mr Keriss

I have been passed your email below from our customer services department and would like to re-emphasize that it is not our intention or practise to fob any of our customers off. Kim is correct when he advises that your sale of contract is with the retailer you bought the sleeping bag from – they need to assess the item in question before deciding whether to take this up with us. If there is manufacturing fault then we will take up the matter – however we cannot offer refunds or compensation directly back to consumers not having gone through the correct channels. I am very confident in the quality of our products and we ensure they go through stringent quality control checks during production – the Lynx has been in our range for over 5 years and performed excellently during this time. I am disappointed to hear of your ordeal and would advise you take this up asap with the place of purchase and ask them to contact us with the product / their opinion. We need to go through correct procedures to draw a conclusion from this one

Regards
Nick Langdon, Product Director

65. Meatfeast

From: Pat Keriss
To: Bury Black pudding company
Subject: Black pudding

How can you justify having a product shaped like a 'member/phallus' and call it a 'black pudding'. I believe this is racist and has no place in today's multi cultural society. To have a product you sell openly designed on a black man's penis is a disgrace. I myself am married to a black man so please don't tell me I do not know what such a phallus looks/tastes like. Please (attempt to) explain yourselves?

NO RESPONSE

66. Softly does it

From: Pat Keriss
To: Mattresses world
Subject: Matressworld

I have recently purchased some land in order to construct a new 'theme' park. Whilst looking for a theme, I had a Eureka moment. Introducing 'Matressworld!'. The idea is simple. To have a number of mattress themed rides, a cafe where everyone sits on mattresses, soft play areas (using mattresses), mattress slides etc etc....

I'm sure you'll agree it's a wonderful idea. I however am after a sponsor to donate a number of high spec mattresses. Could we meet and discuss the possibility of you sponsoring me with around 2500 mattresses? In return I will display your adverts around the theme park. I am sure this could triple your turnover, if not double it.

Kind regard

Pat Keriss

NO RESPONSE

67. Bouncy bouncy

From: Pat Keriss
To: Trampolines World
Subject: Injury

I recently purchased a 6ft trampoline from you.

I am currently sitting here now with a broken collar bone as well as scratches and lacerations to my thigh/ genital region.

I do not exercise regularly (I am currently 28 stone); having lost a lot of weight (I used to be 32 stone). Whilst jumping, one of the springs came apart and I fell with my body through the gap, this catapulted me over the side into the flowerbed/ wall.

I not only broke a bone, but I had shorts on and landed sitting down in a huge patch of stinging nettles. The rash around my groin has subsided with the aid of calamine lotion, however the broken bone persists.

Although I don't work as employers are 'sizist', I would like a payment off you for my injuries. Please tell me how much you are willing to pay and I will send my bank details should this be satisfactory to me.

Pat Keriss

NO RESPONSE

68. Off the scale

From: Pat Keriss
To: The tropical tank
Subject: Catfish

Hi Sean,

I would like some advice?

I recently purchased a few catfish as I read they were a delicacy and I wanted to produce something different for my girlfriend who was coming over for a meal. I fried them gently for about 5 minutes in butter and seasoned them to taste, prior to adding some cumin and fish stock. I served them on a bed of Couscous.

Quite frankly they were disgusting and made us both vomit. My girlfriend even vomited on my chest whilst we lay stricken in bed. It was distressing for us both.

The aquarium is refusing to refund my money claiming that these fish are not for eating (which is laughable I know).

What would you advise re: getting my monies back?

many thanks

Pat Keriss

NO RESPONSE

69. Roper

From: Pat Keriss
To: Ropeloft
Subject: Pubirope

Hi,

I have designed a new type of rope that is twice as strong as normal rope and doesn't chafe the skin should you rub hard down its length.

It is called the 'Pubirope'.

It is basically made from weaving and bonding human (genital) hair together. It is bio degradable, extremely strong and aesthetically pleasing.

It can take a while to produce and is not cheap due to the materials concerned.

Would you like me to send a sample for you to peruse prior to meeting/ you stocking the Pubirope?

Regards

Pat Keriss

**From: Ropeloft
To: Pat Keriss
Subject: Pubirope**

NO!

From: Pat Keriss
To: Ropeloft
Subject: Pubirope

What the hell is wrong with you people?

Your Rope snobs. You think your hemp and shoulders above the rest of us do you? How rude.
Pat Keriss

70. Hoarhouse

From: Pat Keriss
To: Hoar Cross hotel
Subject: treatment enquiry

Hi,

I am looking at staying with 'the lads' for a weekend at your spa/ hotel.

Can you tell me how much your hoars cost for an hour/ night booking? Also, are they into more kinky stuff? I have a friend who is into watching defecations take place whilst he lies under a coffee table looking up through the glass...would your girls be up for this?

Also, are they into LHA (lubricated hand action), group/ bdsm/ strap on etc etc?

I look forward to your reply.

Many thanks

Pat Keriss

NO RESPONSE

71. It'll cost ya

From: Pat Keriss
To: Shaftesbury Garage
Subject: Car quote

Hi,

I'm hoping you can give me a quote? I recently purchased a fantastic car: A Vauxhall Vectra on a 53 plate. It needs some work doing.....it has 1 door missing so will require a replacement, has no front wheels, the chassis needs some welding and I think I may need an engine rebuild. In addition the bonnet needs respraying and I have a leak from the head gasket area.

I am looking to get the car through an MOT next month and wanted a rough quote...I'm guessing it will cost around £70-90 including parts and labour?

Many thanks

Pat Keriss

From: Shaftesbury Garage
To: Pat Keriss
Subject: car quote

Morning Pat. I need the vehicle here so I can price the job properly for you as it req welding and other bodywork. Give me a call 0208 449 9111

From: Pat Keriss
To: Shaftesbury Garage
Subject: car quote

I can't. It's fucked....hence I need your expertise.

If you can pop over and take a look there's an extra £5 in it for you...

Regards
Pat

72. Party time

From: Pat Keriss
To: BNP (London)
Subject: Membership application

Hi

I am looking at joining you having been a long term supporter. I have a query though....I am married to a Jamaican man currently in prison for drug dealing, money laundering, robbery and fraud. He also supports your cause however and sees himself as an honourary Englishman. Would it prove problematic if we both join and he also attends meetings/ rallies on his release?

He is a changed man having commenced attending bible classes a few weeks ago and giving up crack cocaine 2 months ago.

Regards

Pat Keriss

NO RESPONSE

73. Feeling sheepish

From: Pat Keriss
To: Willows farm
Subject: Animal tragic

I visited with my child today and was disgusted. Whilst walking past the sheep/ rams, one of the male sheep had testes hanging down nearly to the floor. My daughter asked what it was and I had to respond 'bags of shopping'.

Having been put in this awkward situation speaking about such matters with a young child (she is only 14), I was then shocked to turn around and see the male ram become visibly aroused and 'enter' a sheep from behind. Again I had to lie and say that the ram was 'looking for somewhere to pack away the shopping'.

I suggest if your animals are frisky you hide them away from young, impressionable and inquisitive eyes! Failing that provide adequate warnings/ signage. You should be ashamed of yourselves.

From: Willows farm
To: Pat Keriss
Subject: Animal tragic

Dear Pat
Thank you for your email dated 27th September with reference to your visit to Willows Farm Village on the same day. We are sorry that you felt you were put in an awkward position with your daughter, as it is never our intention to cause any distress to our visitors. However as a farm with live animals it is possible that visitors will see all aspects of their natural behaviour which provides opportunities to educate our visitors about the countryside and farming life.
Indeed one of our most popular events is our February Frolics event where visitors have the opportunity to see new born lambs and learn about how their mothers then tends to them.

**I wanted to respond to let you know that your comments have been received and to again reiterate that it is never our intention to cause any offence.
Yours sincerely
Carol Blower, Marketing Manager**

From: Pat Keriss
To: Willows Farm
Subject: Disabled nappy change

Further to my previous complaint about animals copulating publicly, I thought I would give Willows another chance today.

Again, I was appalled by what I saw. I wanted to change my baby boy's nappy. The only area available however was a room which had a sign on it reading 'Disabled Nappy Changing'.

So....let me get this straight...only disabled children deserve the right to have their nappies changed but able bodied babies don't?? Your happy to leave able bodied babies in the own faeces all afternoon, whilst disabled children are treated like royalty?

This is prejudice and an absolute disgrace.
Pat Keriss

74. Errol

From: Pat Keriss
To: Barnet Times
Subject: The Barnet Beast

Dear Ms. Lowe,

I read your story entitled 'world's biggest rodent spotted in Totteridge' with interest. I believe I may be able to shed some light....

I have a Silver Grey Syrian Hamster called Errol that I take for exercise around Darlands Lake.

I believe the man who reported this story to you was the man I saw making a hasty retreat when he spotted Errol going about his business.

I usually let him wander a bit as it is a long while since he proved problematic to other wildlife (besides his bullying behaviour toward my Sons (now deceased) gerbil).

I have had a chuckle with Errol regarding his being called the 'Barnet Beast!'

Pat Keriss

From: Barnet Times
To: Pat Keriss
Subject: The Barnet Beast

Hi Pat,

Interesting... though suspect, unless Errol has been on the steroids recently, that he is perhaps a little undersized to compete with the mighty capybara.

I would like to include your alternative view in a follow-up article, however, if you don't mind! If not, please could you send across your age and the road where you live?

Many thanks, Rebecca

From: Pat Keriss
To: Barnet Times
Subject: The Barnet Beast

Hi Rebecca

Silver Grey Syrians are rather large hamsters! Larger than your average run of the mill domestic version that seem to be in vogue these days.

I live in Barnet...Greenhill Parade and I am 55.......I look forward to reading your prose.

Errol is still chuckling at your piece, as am I....thankyou!

Regards

Pat

From: Pat Keriss
To: The Barnet Times
Subject: The Barnet Beast

I opened the paper this week Rebecca with baited breath and saw that I was not mentioned.

Shame. I was quite looking forward to a little local celebrity, as was Errol!

Oh well...!

Pat Keriss

75. What a wanker

From: Pat Keriss
To: Guinness book of world records
Subject: Longest continuous masturbation attempt

I would like to improve troop morale in Afghanistan where I have a number of service personnel friends. We all are single and take a healthy interest in masturbation and the art of self love. I would like to put my experience to the test in undertaking the longest masturbation attempt ever. I reckon (with 15 minute breaks twice a day) I could continue for about 5 days. I believe that I may require some medical assistance after about day 3 due to possible chafing complications, but the pain would be worth it to see the encouragement on my friends faces. I may also collect for a STD charity too.

I will attempt this record alone sitting on a comfortable (pig/cow skin) armchair in the social area of one of the forces bases. I am doing this for my friends and for the sense of achievement I will feel upon completion.

From: Guinness World Records
To: Pat Keriss
Subject: Longest continuous masturbation attempt

The exact title of the record is subject to change and GWR may offer you a valid alternative record if your suggestion is not acceptable.

Until you read and accept all sections of this Agreement, GWR in no way encourages, authorises or permits any Record Attempt to be carried out and we will have absolutely no connection with or authorise any Record Attempt carried out before such acknowledgement.

From: Guinness World Records
To: Pat Keriss
Subject: Longest continuous masturbation attempt

Dear Mr Pat Keriss,

Thank you for sending us the details of your recent record attempt for 'Longest continuous masturbation attempt'. We are afraid to say that we are unable to accept this as a Guinness World Record.

We receive over 60,000 enquiries a year from which only a small proportion are approved by our experienced researchers to establish new categories. These are not 'made up' to suit an individual proposal, but rather 'evolve' as a result of international competition in a field, which naturally accommodates superlatives of the sort that we are interested in. We think you will appreciate that we are bound to favour those that reflect the greatest interest.

Guinness World Records has absolute discretion as to which Guinness World Record applications are accepted and our decision is final. Guinness World Records may at its discretion and for whatever reason identify some records as either no longer monitored by Guinness World Records or no longer viable.

As your record application has not been accepted, Guinness World Records is in no way associated with the activity relating to your record proposal and we in no way endorse this activity. If you choose to proceed with this activity then this is will be of your own volition and at your own risk.

Once again thank you for your interest in Guinness World Records.

Yours sincerely,

Mariamarta Ruano-Graham
Records Management Team

From: Pat Keriss
To: Guinness
Subject: Longest continuous masturbation attempt

Dear Mariamata,

This record is of 'great interest' to counessoirrs of masturbation (myself included) as well as sex industry workers.

I am continuing with this attempt and I will be placing the Words 'New Guinness world record attempt' on all press releases and documentation. I am over riding you on this one as I know that it will be great publicity for Guinness. Just trust me...I know what I'm doing.

Thanks for taking the time to e mail me back. I will be thinking of you as I attempt to break the record.

Regards

Pat

76. Sure got a perdy mouth aint he?

From: Pat Keriss
To: NHS Direct
Subject: Swine Flu

I phoned your service earlier today and was given short thrift by your member of staff.

I enquired as to a hypothetical question. If I had a friend who had been drunk and had intercourse with a pig whilst camping overnight on a working farm, then developed flu like symptoms, do you think this could be swine flu? Can it be contracted in this manner?

This was, although a strange question, a serious one nonetheless, and one to which I would desperately like the answer to ASAP.

Many thanks

From: NHS Direct
To: Pat Keriss
Subject: Swine flu

We are not aware of any data covering the transmission of pandemic influenza ("swine flu") by sexual intercourse with pigs. We have attached a link showing the normal transmission route.

If your friend currently has symptoms which he would like to discuss with a nurse, please encourage him to call NHS Direct on 0845 4647. For patients' safety, all calls are recorded. NHS Direct is open 24 hours a day, 7 days a week. If he thinks that he may have swine flu, he should contact the National Pandemic Flu Service (see second link)

http://www.who.int/csr/resources/publications/Adviceusemaskscommunityrevised.pdf
http://www.direct.gov.uk/en/Swineflu/DG_177831
Kind regards,
The NHS Direct Contact Us Team

From: Pat Keriss
To: NHS Direct
Subject: Swine flu

I have phoned him and he extremely relieved...many thanks!

He did have another question though...he wondered if (hypothetically) a small rodent type creature, such as a hamster, were to lick a substance (such as jam) from his genital region and he accidentally got a 'nick' on his manhood from the rodents claws, is this dangerous and could it cause infection?

Many thanks

77. A huge joke

From: Pat Keriss
To: The Scottish FA
Subject: Shame to the nation

Hello,
I am hoping you can help?

I am writing a book entitled 'shame to the nation' which explains the effect underachieving/ embarrassing football teams have on national confidence.

As the Scottish team can be classed in that camp, and hence the national psyche is one of 'perennial losers', would George Burley agree to giving a quote explaining why he thinks Scotland are such a poor footballing, clichéd gallant braveheart, always the bridesmaid, never the bride, nearly men?

I look forward to your reply

Pat Keriss

From: The Scottish FA
To: Pat Keriss
Subject: Shame to the nation

Pat

Now that is hilarious. You would like us to put up the National Manager to explain why our football is so embarrassing....?!

I've heard it all now.

I think that you can safely assume that this is a resounding no.

Rob

Rob Shorthouse, Head of Communications
The Scottish Football Association

From: Pat Keriss
To: Rob Shorthouse, Scottish FA
Subject: Shame to the nation

Dear Rob

I am confused?

The request is merely for Mr Burley to comment on other people's viewpoint that the Scottish national team are on a par with an English Conference side. This is not my opinion, but that of the English population as a whole according to independent research.

Are you saying that he is under the illusion that the Scottish national team are a football superpower?

Can I quote you on that?

Regards

Pat Keriss

From: Rob Shorthouse, Scottish FA
To: Pat Keriss
Subject: Shame to the nation

That is not what I am saying. You can quote me on this though... 'Yours is the most ridiculous interview request that this office has received in quite some time.'

But thanks for writing in...

Rob

From: Pat Keriss
To: Rob Shorthouse, Scottish FA
Subject: Shame to the nation

Rob...

This should suffice?

At least the Scottish took the claims made seriously, with their Head of Communications, Rob Shorthouse asking if they could '....put up the national manager to explain why our football is so embarrassing...'. The author, Pat Keriss declined, to save accusations of anti scottish bias.

Cheers for all your help

Pat

From: Rob Shorthouse, Scottish FA
To: Pat Keriss
Subject: Shame to the nation

You are my hero! Make sure you send us a copy of this incredible article.

Rob Shorthouse
Head of Communications

From: Pat Keriss
To: Rob Shorthouse, Scottish FA
Subject: Shame to the nation

After the 'bravehearts' 2-0 capitulation to those footballing world superpowers, Japan, on Saturday, is George Burley now willing to speak to me regarding the immense shame that he, and the 'football' team, has heaped on an already downtrodden nation?

Pat Keriss

From: Rob Shorthouse, Scottish FA
To: Pat Keriss
Subject: Shame to the nation

Pat

Great to hear from you again.

Please do continue to write. We all enjoy your emails so much.

Rob

From: Pat Keriss
To: Rob Shorthouse, Scottish FA
Subject: Shame to the nation

Dear Rob,

I'll take your comments as backhanded flattery although I sense a hint of dourness to your tone?

I am getting the impression this interview with Burley is never going to happen. I can live with that but am hoping you can fulfil 2 minor requests instead of the interview...

Would George comment on what he thinks has gone wrong since that heady day on the 5th September of beating Macedonia 2-0?

The second request is that I am sent a signed Scotland shirt for my cousin? Christmas is coming up and it would be a nice accompaniment to the Lynx box set he currently has lined up for him.

Cheers

Pat

From: Pat Keriss
To: Rob Shorthouse, Scottish FA
Subject: Shame to the nation

Dear Rob

Sorry it seems like ages since I wrote, but I haven't heard from you for a while?

The article is coming on great thanks although I imagine things aren't too rosy in the Scottish FA garden after yet another humiliation yesterday to Wales of all people. By all accounts they were unlucky. Unlucky to only win 3-0 and not by more if my sources are correct.

Anyhow...I wondered if the Scotland team would like a warm up match next Summer against a team for whom a friend plays? He plays for St Albans and they are willing to play at home and split the gate receipts with you guys? Scotland would start at slight underdogs at 3-1. I think ill have a few quid on the draw though at 2-1 as this will be at the tail end of a long St Albans season and anything could happen.

Let me know your thoughts.

Regards as ever

Pat

From: Rob Shorthouse, Scottish FA
To: Pat Keriss
Subject: Shame to the nation

I no longer work for the Scottish FA.

78. Overpaid, underworked planks

From: Pat Keriss
To: London Underground
Subject: Lost bag

My lost bag contained a black dildo, 4 rabbit vibrators, cuffs, love beads, whips, cock rings, anal love eggs and lubrication.

I am concerned that the staff you employ lack common sense and decency. I would like this back UNUSED by your staff.

Pat Keriss

From: London Underground
To: Pat Keriss
Subject: Lost bag

Dear Mr keriss

Thank you for your enquiry about Lost Property.

We are sorry to inform you that we have been unable to locate the property that was lost.

Yours sincerely

Lost Property Office
Transport for London
200 Baker Street

From: Pat Keriss
To: London Underground
Subject: Lost bag

So it's taken you a month to see if you have my property? In other words it's given your thieving staff a month to take my goods and chattels and hide the evidence away.

£40,000 a year to sit there, sneer at customers and do fu*k all. And that's for a maximum of 12 hours per week 'work'. Enjoy the cock ring. It might give you something to do on your shift.
Pat Keriss

79. Shit off a shovel

From: Pat Keriss
To: Al Gore (repower America)
Subject: Shitealight

I am a Dr. based in the UK where my current idea is not taken seriously.

I have set up a small woodland based community where all power is produced with human excreta. The excreta not only powers the turbines, generators and windmills, but the apparatus and homesteads are all built used dried and treated human excreta.

Despite a rather unpleasant smell when it rains, the system works fantastically and is a terrific use of filtered raw sewage.

I would love an organisation such as yours to offer their backing to my scheme entitled 'shitealite'.

NO RESPONSE

80. Easy Rider

From: Pat Keriss
To: Discount scooters
Subject: Pimp my ride

Hello,

I recently became seriously injured and I now require the aid of a mobility scooter. Luckily, I am not worried by monetary constraints; however I am worried about the stigma of buying a top of the range scooter.

With that in mind, I have decided I want to buy a TOTR scooter...but I want to customise it.

Is it possible for you to 'pimp' my scooter?

I would like a metallic paint job, go faster stripes, 16" alloys and a calf skin seat.

Please tell me if you have anything like this in stock and the probable cost.

Many thanks

Pat

From: Discount scooters
To: Pat Keriss
Subject: Scooter

Dear Pat

Once you have identified a suitable top of the range scooter that suits your requirements we are able to Pimp it at request
Paint finish to suit
seat covers etc

Cost will be subject to scooter considered paint approx £400.00. seat covers to be sourced and quoted.

From: Pat Keriss
To: Discount scooters
Subject: Scooter

Dear Richard

That's great.

And the alloys?

Also, will you be able to fit a bang and olufsen stereo system with tweeter and woofer?

Regards

Pat

From: Discount Scooters
To: Pat Keriss
Subject: Scooter

Of course.

81. wtf

From: Pat Keriss
To: Literacy trust
Subject: jbo

edwrd igota questun fro yoo if tht ok

?
I AVBENRITTING 4A LOn timnow butt kanut gitajoob. uavany thin ther 4me?

pat

NO RESPONSE

82. Hound dog

From: Pat Keriss
To: Camelot castle (Cornwall)
Subject: Gashy

Hello

I am extremely excited by your upcoming doggie ball! I have a few questions prior to booking my stay if you are agreeable and discreet enough to answer them for me?

I would like to book a room for myself and the person closest to me in the world...my dog 'Gashy'. Would it be possible to ensure our room has the petals of a hundred roses scattered on the bed and his favourite song playing when we enter the room? The song is 'I would do anything for love, but I won't do that'.

I would also like the room to be stocked with scented bubble bath, some meat paste, some KY jelly (Gashy gets chapped skin) and a couple of Lassie DVD's.

This is an opportunity for us to spend some quality time together. I hope you can appreciate this and do your utmost to help myself and Gashy bond as much as is humanly possible.

Kind Regards

Pat Keriss

NO RESPONSE

83. Tweet tweet bang

From: Pat Keriss
To: RSPB
Subject: Parakeets

I have a problem with rose ringed parakeets in my garden. There are hundreds of them. I have taken to exterminating them and I now have shot around 80 with a high powered air rifle. I have a problem though...disposal of the bodies.

Is it possible to send an operative over to collect and dispose of the Parakeet bodies as they are starting to make my she'd 'kick up' a bit to be honest.

Many thanks

Pat Keriss

NO RESPONSE

84. Van Goch

From: Pat Keriss
To: Derby County FC
Subject: Dickov doll

Hi Dawn

I have manufactured a thousand man dolls based on Paul Dickov.

The idea is simple, the dolls have a 'phallus' that is velcroed on and can be pulled off. Once pulled off, the doll makes the noise 'ooooowwww! Now I'm Paul Dickov!'...A novel product and a clever play on words I'm sure you'll agree?

The dolls have been selling very well and I have sold around 400 of them. With that in mind I have a quick query.....if I send some in, would Paul mind signing them for me? If so I reckon I can double the price charged once I knock up a 'certificate of authenticity'.

Many Thanks

Pat Keriss

From: Derby County FC
To: Pat Keriss
Subject: Dickov doll

Hi,

Can you please send me a sample.

Kind regards
Dawn Spendlove
Marketing manager

From: Pat Keriss
To: Derby County FC
From: Pat Keriss
Subject: Dickov doll

Hi Dawn

No Worries.....would you like to pay cash or cheque?

Regards

Pat

From: Derby County FC
To: Pat Keriss
Subject: Dickov doll

Hi,

I will return it just want to see what product you would like us to endorse as our retail manager will need to see the actual item.

Thanks

Dawn

From: Pat Keriss
To: Derby County FC
Subject: Dickov doll

Hi Dawn,

That all sounds well and good, however I don't want you to steal the idea to be frank.

If you purchase one then at least I will see some return. I will offer 20% discount if you want to buy more than 5. I can't say fairer than that...

Regards
Pat

From: Derby County FC
To: Pat Keriss
Subject: Dickov doll

Hi,

We have discussed this and for Paul to endorse this he will need to see one.

I will assure you we would never steal this as it is not a product we would ever want to produce it simply doesn't fit with our brand.

I trust this email with alleviate any concerns you may have and if Paul does agree to sign some of the products it would obviously increase the price for you.

If you could therefore send a sample I will review with Paul and ensure it is returned to you unused, boxed etc in the condition was received in.

Kind regards

Dawn

From: Pat Keriss
To: Derby County FC
Subject: Dickov doll

Hi Dawn,

Sorry...I have been stung before....by QPR. I designed a Danny Shittu doll that, when bent in half, screamed' I'm having a Danny Shi* ooooooooo!'. Unbelievably they weren't happy and even threatened legal action. Outrageous I know.

Don't worry...I'll just carry on selling them anyway and try not to put too much more on the packaging regarding being a DCFC authentic product etc...

Regards

Pat

From: Derby County FC
To: Pat Keriss
Subject: Dickov doll

Hi,

Could you please email me your phone number and I'll give you a call to discuss further.

Kind regards

Dawn

From: Pat Keriss
To: Derby County FC
Subject: Dickov doll

Hi Dawn

If you do not want to spend the money to purchase one, then the only reason for a phone call would be personal. I am afraid however that I am married...I am sure you are a lovely woman, but I am afraid the last time I 'played an away game', the wife found out and I awoke to a meat cleaver flirting with my never regions.

With her varied moods, travelling family relations and drink problems, I am never revisiting that place again.

Maybe you could try www.match.com; I hear that has quite a success ratio no matter what you are looking for?

From: Derby County FC
To: Pat Keriss
Date: Monday 19th October 2009
Subject: Dickov doll

Hi Pat,

You have completely misunderstood, if you could you call me as need to discuss this product with you. My numbers are below.
Regards, Dawn

85. Isnt that a peach?

From: Pat Keriss
To: Del Monte
Subject: Man melon

Hi,

I have invented a new product that I would be interested in Del Monte marketing for me. Introducing....the 'Man Melon'.

As you are aware, a number of single men/ sexual deviants in the UK use melons for gratification. By that token, I have produced a melon that has a phallus shaped hole in it allowing the man to use the melon in a sexual manner without spoiling irreparably the contents of the melon. Once used it can simply be rinsed out and placed in the fridge for use by guests/ visitors.

It is dual use. This fills a huge gap in the market and has taken me a few years to develop and 'road test'. At first the results were messy and resulted in fruit spoilage. I have now ironed out all problems and it works like a dream. It's just like being with a real woman, except it's cheaper. And less grief.

I am more than happy to come and demonstrate the 'Man Melon' to you in the first instance as I am sure you will be blown away by the design.

Regards

Pat Keriss

NO RESPONSE

86. Crap hole

From: Pat Keriss
To: Luton town FC programme
Subject: Luton's not all bad

Hi Andrew

I would like to offer my assistance to redress the balance with regard to Luton's poor image.

As you know, it has a reputation as a poor, crowded, smelly, dirty, noisy, excreta ridden, outdated, past its sell by date, lower working class, scummy, dangerous, violent, crime ridden, poverty stricken, grey, poorly housed, concrete hell hole.

On the plus side it has a few nice food takeaways and it's near the M1.

I just thought it was time someone redressed the balance.

Pat Keriss

(Please feel free to include this piece in the programme).

From: Luton Town FC Programme
To: Pat Keriss
Subject: Luton's not all bad

Are you the editor of the Crap Towns Guide?

I'm pleased you took the time to visit the site and email me.

Best wishes

Andrew
Press Officer
Luton Town FC

87. Shergar's last stand

From: Pat Keriss
To: Goodwood racing course
Subject: Equine dining

I recently pur-chased a business from France called Ecouter cuisine which roughly translates as 'equine cuisine'. As a gastronome and fine diner of many years experience, take it from me that there is no finer meat on god's earth than that of the horse. Our mobile van stocks the highest quality horse meat available in gyros and pita bread and is received very well at country fairs within the country set.

We offer novelty ranges too including 'steak drizzled in red rum', the 'Shergar sizzler' and a simple white horse meat mousse called 'desert orchid'.

Please could you inform me as to how to go about gaining a concession to offer my Equine dining products at horse racing meets?

Regards

Pat Keriss

To: Pat Keriss
From: Goodwood Race course
Subject: Equine dining

Dear Mr Keriss,

Many thanks for your email. Unfortunately I don't think that your service will be suitable for our horseracing meetings, I fear that our customers and members won't want to eat horse meat.

With best wishes,
Chiara

To: Goodwood race course
From: Pat Keriss
Subject: Equine dining

Dear Chiara

Don't let fear rule your life. Let the public decide. If your customers are happy to watch the horses be whipped, starved and mistreated like they are at Goodwood, then I am positive they will not object to the odd 'comply or die horse pie'.......

Please can I have the contact details of the organ grinder who judges such matters...?

Pat Keriss

88. Custard creamed

To: Burtons Biscuits
From: Pat Keriss
Subject: Bourbon laced biscuits

On a recent night out meeting some rugger friends I had the misfortune to eat half a packet of your 'Bourbon' biscuits. Although my friends were drinking heavily, I remained on Coca-Cola as I am teetotal.

The next morning however I awoke with an obese woman by my side and the sorest drumming noise in my head that I have ever experienced.

Being a married man I was beside myself as I have never cheated on my wife. Upon admitting my indiscretion to her, she left me and I am now sleeping on a colleagues Argos sofabed (which is not renowned for comfort, let me tell you).

To cut to the quick, I believe that you have acted extremely irresponsibly by selling biscuits laced with Bourbon whisky whilst not even bothering to issue any alcoholic content warning on the packet.

I have now lost my wife, my dignity and have started drinking whisky by the bottle all caused by that blasted half packet of Burtons Bourbons.

I demand you place a warning on your packets with immediate effect and I would be interested to learn how you intend to recompense me for this outrageous oversight?

Pat Keriss

NO RESPONSE

89. Bolt from the blue

From: Pat Keriss
To: Usain Bolt management
Subject: The Usain bolt

Hello,

I am a huge fan of Usain Bolt. To that end I have designed and manufactured a product that I have been selling here in the UK and I am about to offer worldwide. Not only does this product provide me with a (more than) comfortable income, but it also raises the profile of Usain so everyone is a winner!

The product is simple. It is a 'Usain bolt' that is sold in builder's merchants and DIY stores. It bears the likeness of Usain undertaking his celebration and has proved a huge hit with the construction fraternity who are also huge athletics fans.

My query is simple; would Usain like to purchase some 'Usain bolts' for use around his houses? I am prepared to offer a 40% discount if he purchases more than 50 packets (of 6 bolts). These currently wholesale at £10 per packet. Usain will therefore receive £500 (wholesale) of 'Usain bolts' for only £300 which is a great deal! The retail price would be in the region of £1000.

I look forward to your reply

Pat Keriss

NO RESPONSE

90. Give peas a chance

From: Pat Keriss
To: Birds eye
Subject: Her Peas

I have invented a new 'pea' which I would like to offer to Birds Eye.

The idea is to increase the proliferation of females eating peas on a daily basis. The health benefits are immense with just one serving of freshly frozen garden peas and petit pois containing as much vitamin C as two large apples, more fibre than a slice of wholemeal bread and more thiamine than a pint of whole milk.

To have more females (especially whose in the family way) consuming peas can therefore only be a good thing.

Introducing the 'Her Peas'.

Her Peas will have slightly different coloration with a tinge of pink to the outer shell. They will also be sprayed with the smell of Roses and the pack will also show recipes for the person who is the main cook in the most families: the woman.

They can also be cooked as part of a romantic meal by the woman's boyfriend/ lover/ husband (delete as appropriate). Imagine the scene....mood music playing, a bottle of red and the gentleman friend presenting his special lady with a steaming plate of Her Peas.

I look forward to discussing my invention in further detail in the near future and I await your response with vigour.

Regards

Pat Keriss

<u>NO RESPONSE</u>

91. Felling hothothot

From: Pat Keriss
To: Cherished radiators
Subject: The Gaydiator

Hello

I have a new product invention that I would like to offer you for sale. I am sure you will agree it will be huge (especially to the homosexual radiator buying market).

Introducing 'The Gaydiator'.

The Gaydiator works as a normal radiator with regards to it heats rooms. This item however has a few subtle differences. Firstly they are coloured pink. Secondly (and this is the unique selling point), as it heats up it 'talks'.

I have approached Dale Winton and Alan Carr to do the voiceover. Winton at present wants too much money and I believe Carr's profile is better and he is the current cream of the homosexual crop.

I digress....as the Gaydiator heats up it firstly whispers (in a camp voice) 'I'm getting hot'. After a few more degrees it says in a sultry tone 'I'm hotter now'. After 5 more of these heat induced interjections it ends with a crescendo (every 2 minutes) of 'mmmmmmm...I'm steaming!'.

In addition to the obvious USP, there will be a volume control on the Gaydiator for use at night.

I am excited with the probability of you stocking this product and I await further instruction.

Pat Keriss

From: Cherished radiators
To: Pat Keriss
Subject: The Gaydiator

Send me a picture please

From: Pat Keriss
To: Cherished radiators
Subject: The Gaydiator

Sorry...I do not have any pictures as I make them to order and I am still awaiting my first sale.

Imagine a normal looking radiator, but pink and with heat sensors and a glued on voicebox (and walkman speakers attached to the side) and you'll get the picture.

I have another one in design stage: The 'Hawkingator'. Again, it has heat sensors but when it heats up it lets out a voice based on Dr Stephen Hawing that says 'I'm hot'. 'I'm still hot'and 'ouch...this burns like a motherfuc*ker'.

If you order a few I can send you a picture down prior to sending it?

Pat Keriss

92. Charlotte

From: Pat Keriss
To: Bunyan church, Stevenage
Subject: Weekly service

Hi Sir,

I am moving to Stevenage in the next few weeks and I hoping you can assist me with some advice?

Although a Baptist, I have not been to church for many years due to my Tourette's. Unlike most sufferers, my tic is that of the stereotype: I swear incessantly, very loudly at the most inopportune moments.

These words and insults have left me socially outcast save for my family. I shout comments about female genitalia, I call people the most unpleasant names and I shout the F and C words frequently.

My query is simple though...would you object to my attending your services once a week?

God bless

Pat Keriss

From: Bunyan Church, Stevenage
To: Pat Keriss
Subject: Weekly service

Dear Pat

I'm so sorry not to have answered this email before now.

What a difficult problem! Why don't we meet and discuss ways of including you in community worship?

I hope your move goes well and that God blesses you in your new home,

Dave

From: Pat Keriss
To: Bunyan Church, Stevenage
Subject: Weekly service

Dear Sir Dave,

I am afraid I will not be able to meet....I am very awkward in one to one social interactions. It exacerbates my tic and I would swear and spit at you sadly. I have also been known to have urinary leaks when I feel under pressure.

I understand you're not wanting to include me in your flock.

I wish you all the best and I will continue my prayers in the confines of my own bedsit.

All the best

Pat

From: Bunyan Church, Stevenage
To: Pat Keriss
Subject: Weekly service

Dear Pat

If I can quote you: "I understand your not wanting to include me in your flock." I have no idea where you got that impression! It simply isn't true. As pastor I have to enter into relationship with people, regardless of label, to encourage them in the Christian faith, so the offer to meet is still there, in spite of the tics.

When's good for you?

Dave

93. Feeling chuffed

From: Pat Keriss
To: Hastings Direct Insurance
Subject: World record insurance

Hello

I have a strange (but totally serious) request.

I earn my living as an adult film star and have appeared in many famous adult films (including 'Night Rider', 'Fanny Batter' and 'Fast on the farm with Jansen Mutton').

I am soon to be attempting a world porn film record but I require some insurance. I intend to be, in American Football parlance, the 'receiver' and have full unprotected anal sex with 100 men within a 24 hour period.

Please can you inform me as to whether you will insure me in the unlikely event I contract a sexual illness. Also, I would like some damage cover should I suffer from cuts/ chafing that render me unable to walk/ work for a few weeks.

Please inform me of the quote ASAP for my world record attempt as I need to get cracking.

Kind regards.

Pat Keriss

NO RESPONSE

94. Beyonce

From: Pat Keriss
To: Nick Knowles.com
Subject: Nick Knowles fan club

Hi Nick

I am your biggest fan...bar none! I have followed your career lovingly since you first started out and have now (I believe) every single programme you have ever recorded on tape including all the old DIY SOS which I still watch now to cheer me up.

I have a spare room which I use as my 'Nick Knowles room' where I have thousands of pictures and videos of you...like I said I really am your number 1 fan! I have turned a number of friends on to you as well and we have had a few (unofficial) Nick Knowles afternoons and the NKCM (Nick Knowles coffee morning) where we watch a show or two of yours and swap our favourite NK stories.

To cut a long story short...I would love to start up a fan club dedicated to the best presenter this country has ever seen without exception, which I will run and lovingly attend to...what are your thoughts?

I would run a monthly newsletter; produce a range of NK memorabilia (key rings, branded tools and hammers and maybe a calendar). Obviously all profits would go directly to you.

Keep making us happy Nick; it's why you were put on god's earth. You are a gift from heaven.

All my love, Pat xx

NO RESPONSE

95. Slyxdexic

From: Pat Keriss
To: Daily Mirror
Date: Monday 12th October 2009
Subject: Steeven Gattly

Dear Rankin

Altho dylsexic, I can still reed and rite.
 Steeven gatly dyed yetseday and you repart tht 'he dyed of drinkin minge'.

He is gayy! Why yoo rite thiss?

Pat

NO RESPONSE

96. Smoking a fag

From: Pat Keriss
To: Tesco
Subject: Appalled by Tesco!

I am appalled!

As a homosexual of 8 years experience, I could not believe the name of one of your products when I shopped yesterday with my close friend, Bryce.

After we had chosen our items and before we packed the milk, coffee, tea and fudge, we decided to browse the frozen items.

I was flabbergasted that you have a product called 'faggots' for sale on the shelves! Bryce seemed to laugh it off and said it was normal. I disagreed and we had our first lovers tiff (although the making up was gentle and loving). I digress...how dare you offer a product called 'faggots'. It is totally offensive to homosexuals and it is no wonder gay bashing still exists in this country....I lay the suffering endured by the gay community firmly at Tesco's door after seeing this product!

Whatever next? A fish product called Lesbo's? A Drink called rimming? A pie called the felcher??

A disgrace!

Pat Keriss

From: Tesco
To: Pat Keriss
Subject: Appalled by Tesco

Dear Pat,

Thank you for your email. Firstly, please allow me to apologise for the delay in getting back to you. We do endeavour to get back to all customer enquiries as quickly and efficiently as possible, and I am very sorry that we've let you down in this respect.

I'm sorry to learn that you were offended by the presence of faggots on our shelves. I can understand that due to the current slang interpretation of the word, that you would be upset at seeing this in store, especially as you've been homosexual for at least eight years.

Please be assured that we would never intentionally insult any of our customers in this manner, but I'm afraid that the term faggot in this instance refers to a spicy meatball. This is a traditional food item that has been in circulation for far longer than the slang term that you refer to in your email. A faggot is also a small bundle of twigs; however I suspect that we do not sell this product in any of our stores, considering you can literally pick them off the ground.

I will certainly make our Buying team aware of your concerns concerning the name of the spicy meatballs you were appalled with, so that they can take it up with the relevant people and may even take it all the way to the European Parliament, as we are committed to making sure our customers feel comfortable while packing their milk, coffee, tea and fudge in Tesco.

I'm sorry for any distress caused when you noticed this on our shelves, and thank you for taking the time to make me aware of this. I hope that you and Bryce have made up properly after your first tiff. If you have any further queries please do not hesitate to contact me quoting TES6906061X. Kind Regards
James Brownell, Customer Service Manager, Tesco

From: Pat Keriss
To: Tesco
Subject: Appalled by Tesco

Dear James Brownell,
Thankyou for your belated reply.
The main Wikipedia entry for fagott is '*Faggot*, often shortened to *fag*, is a pejorative term and common homophobic slur against lesbian, gay, bisexual, and transgender (LGBT) people'. If this is the common use of the word then Tesco should cease persecuting the les, gay, bi and transgender community immediately.
You also 'joke'? That you can 'literally pick them off the ground', when you refer to fagott's. I have had to pick up a number of close friends after such 'gay bashing' incidents. Try telling them of your interpretation and I am sure they would disagree and be mortified by this attitude.
Myself and Bryce are working through our problems, thanks for your concern. He is a lovely man, albeit it a little 'rough' around the edges. I am training him with my experience of the homosexual lifestyle and I hope and pray for a long and loving future together.
Pat Keriss

From: Tesco
To: Pat Keriss
Subject: Appalled by Tesco

Dear Pat,

Thank you for getting back in touch with me. I do appreciate that the term faggot is listed on the beacon of truth that is Wikipedia as a pejorative term. However it also states my points about the spicy meatball being called a faggot for quite a long time in the Midlands, before it was adopted as a slang term for a homosexual person. It also confirms that a faggot is small collection of twigs or branches, amongst other interpretations of the word. As I stated previously, all your points have been logged on our system, so that the relevant people in our business know of your complaint. Thank you for taking the time to write to me and if you have any further queries please do not hesitate to contact me.

97. Catpack furniture

From: Pat Keriss
To: The post office
Subject: Sutcliffe

My cat Shipman recently had some Kittens (called Fred, Rose, Myra and Sutcliffe). I have managed to find loving neighbours to take 3 of the 4, but one of them, Sutcliffe, is to be homed at a friend's home 20 miles away.

Being immobile, I cannot get to the post office. Therefore I packaged Sutcliffe in a shoebox (with airholes) and parcel taped it shut.

On 3 occasions now the postman has refused to take Sutcliffe to be sent to my friend. The tape is too tight to open and I have resorted to pushing small lumps of Kit e cat through the airholes to aid Sutcliffe's sustenance.

The box is now becoming sodden with urine and faeces and I am at the end of my tether.

Is it possible to send a postman over to do as he should and deliver my kitten to my friend?

NO RESPONSE

98. Compact risk

From: Pat Keriss
To: EMI
Subject: Downloads

I recently downloaded a number of your artist's albums from a file sharing site.

Of the 12 I downloaded, 2 of them (Peter Doherty and Kate Perry) did not record/ come out properly.

To make amends, could you please send me copies of the original albums free of charge?

Pat Keriss

From: EMI
To: Pat Keriss
Subject: Downloads

Hi

Please can you tell me what site that you purchased these tracks from?

Thanks
Melanie
EMI Music

From: Pat Keriss
To: EMI
Subject: Downloads

Hi Melanie,
 I didn't purchase them as such. I downloaded them on something called a 'file sharing site' that a Chinese friend who is in the CD/ DVD re-sale industry showed me. Is it possible to replace these albums then? I am especially keen to listen to Pete(r) Doherty's drug addled rantings this weekend as I've a raucous night in planned with my new love. If you pop it in the post first class in the morning I may get it by Saturday?
Pat Keriss

99. Only a squid?

From: Pat Keriss
To: Poundland
Subject: Orange matchmakers

Hi,

I was wondering if you could tell me how much the orange flavoured matchmakers are please?

Thanks

NO RESPONSE

100. Rough diver

From: Pat Keriss
To: British Swimming
Subject: Fundraising event

Hi Joanna

I'm hoping you can point me in the right direction?

I am attempting to raise some money to support a forces friend of mine who got injured in a freak accident (involving his wife, a door handle and some margarine...a long and messy story)....anyhow he is very badly injured and will be off work for around a year and I would like to arrange a benefit along with his army buddies in order to keep him afloat financially.

I digress....my friend, Ryan, has a reputation for being a practical joker as well as a sexual deviant. He is however interested in diving. With that in mind, we would like to hire a diving pool and have a fundraising 'muff diver' evening.

The idea is simple; we will produce a large buoyant 'muff' which will stay on the surface of the pool (weighted down by bricks). In turn the divers have to dive into the muff. As each round goes on, the muff gets smaller and tighter. The person who dives into the smallest muff will win a trophy called the 'muff bucket'.

Please could you look into which pool we could use for this worthwhile event or pass us in the general direction of someone who would OK this fundraiser?

Hopefully with your assistance we can raise e-muff! money for Ryan

Regards

Pat Keriss

From: British Swimming
To: Pat Keriss
Subject: Fundraising event

Hi Pat,
Many thanks for your email.
This is something that the ASA cannot support but if take a look on the http://www.diving-gbdf.com/ **you will see all the diving pool across the UK and their contact details.**
Many thanks,
Becky.

101. Paul Scholes

From: Pat Keriss
To: McDonalds
Subject: Ginge

Whilst visiting an ill relative in Manchester, I popped into McDonalds for lunch. I was served by a northern man who, as soon as he heard my southern accent, sneered.

I bit into my burger and got something stuck between my teeth. I noticed a large ginger pubic hair which I managed to eject. I then bit in again and the same thing happened. I opened the burger and found a total of 16 pubic hairs on my burger.

I spoke to your (ginger haired) northern operative who said that I was 'tasting a piece of northerness' and I should 'be glad to binge on the ginge'. I was appalled. He said the manager was not there and offered me a replacement.

Upon sitting down, I again opened the burger and found another 6 pubic hairs (also ginger). He said that he thought I'd like to be 'fed by the red 'and told me to stop moaning and just eat it.

I am quite frankly shocked by this behaviour and would like a voucher for a bacon double with cheese as recompense at the least.

In all the years I have eaten at McDonalds, I have only found pubic hairs 5 times; this one visit beat the combined total of pubic hairs combined.

NO RESPONSE

102. Stalin

From: Pat Keriss
To: Gordon Ramsey
Subject: Commie chefs

I keep hearing the term 'commie chef'. Can you please explain why all of your chefs have to be communists to work for you? Its nothing short of a disgrace.

Pat Keriss

From: Gordon Ramsey Restaurants
To: Pat Keriss
Subject: Commies chefs

Dear Pat,

Thank you for your email. Commis chef means a trainee chef who has the most junior position in the kitchen. It is derived from the French word commettre to employ, commit. It has no link to commuinism.

Hope this has answered your question.

Kind Regards

Sophie Jenkins
Gordon Ramsay Holdings Limited

103. Puss

From: Pat Keriss
To: The discharge unit, Barnet hospital
Subject: Secretion

Hello

I have an embarrassing discharge and I hope you can give me some advice?

Last year I became heavily involved in the swinging scene with my fiancée (who has now left me for a female member of the swinging fraternity). Anyhow, we were into dangerswinging, an alternative form of swinging where no protection is used.

To cut a fun at first but horrid now story short, for the last few months I have been unfortunate enough to have daily secretions of yellow and greeny coloured puss from my penis. This is becoming a huge problem now as my workmates have commented on my touching my genitalia often (to alleviate the itching), as well as noticing a wet patch from the discharge on cotton, light coloured clothing.

I have also recently split with a new girlfriend who said she loved me but could not stand the smell of the secretion any longer.

Please can I make an appointment to come in and show you my penis and secretion?

Many thanks

Pat Keriss

NO RESPONSE

104. Corporate loop us

From: Pat Keriss
To: Lupus Capital
Subject: Lupus naked run

I'm hoping you can help?

I suffer from Lupus which, as you may know, attacks the immune system. I am looking to arrange a 'naked lupus run' for 5KM in order to raise money for Lupus UK. I would very much like it if you could sponsor us in our naked lupus mission?

Your workers are more than welcome to join in the run although we would prefer (attractive) females to even out the ratio. The run will take place indoors in a London based sports centre and will be covered by the press. This could provide some great coverage for your company.

I look forward to your reply.

From: Lupus Capital
To: Pat Keriss
Subject: Lupus naked run

Dear Mr Keriss

Thank you very much for your email. I am afraid that our charitable budget has been fully expensed at this time and so we are unable to offer financial support. May we wish you the very best of luck with your endeavours.
Lupus Capital plc

From: Pat Keriss
To: Lupus Capital
Subject: Lupus naked run

Dear 'Lupus Capital',

LIES!

Regards
Pat Keriss

105. No place like groan

From: Pat Keriss
To: ITV
Subject: Doc Martin?

I am very upset with the actions of one of your 'actors'.

Recently on a trip to Soho with a close friend, we left a bar called the Jolly Rodger. My friend was ill after he had his drink spiked and was vomiting heavily on the street. He had sick on his clothes and face and his dreadlocks were matted with human bile.

I was worried about him and I looked around for help. I happened to see the actor 'Martin Clunes' coming out of the Jolly and I asked for assistance. He replied 'fu*k off, in mot a doctor' and scuttled off.

In Rocky, Sylvester Stallone trained to be a boxer. In Taxi driver, De Niro knew how to drive a cab. How therefore could Martin Clunes not know basic life saving and first aid procedures?

Lucky my friend recovered with some TLC, however the situation could have been horrendous.

I would suggest you train Mr Clunes who, although he is acting in a low budget, run of the mill 'comedy', should be professional enough to at least want to learn the basics of the medical profession.

I will be selling my 'No Place like Home' video box set on eBay out of protest at his poor attitude in this matter.

From: ITV
To: Pat Keriss
Subject: Doc Martin?

Dear Pat Keriss
Thank you for your email. We have forwarded your concerns to the production team for their consideration.
Kind Regards, ITV Viewer Services

106. Throwing in the trowel

From: Pat Keriss
To: Crocus (Garden catalogue)
Subject: SDS appliances

Hello

I would like to enquire as to a range of gardening products you may/ may not stock?

I am a member of the cottaging and SDS (Sexual deviant society). Myself and other members enjoy gardening and wondered if you have any sexually based novelty items?

In a lull of activity a short while ago, we discussed our 'sexy gardening items' wish list. These included an artificial birds nest shaped like a muff, a phallic shaped fork (with phalluses as the prongs), a pair of Wellington boots with prints of genatalia on and a wheelbarrow with a dildo on the front for use by couples who enjoy making love in the fresh air.

Please inform us as to whether you stock these items or anything similar? We are more than happy to discuss our needs should you wish to plug this gap in the SDS market.

Regards

Pat Keriss

NO RESPONSE

107. The calf mince

From: Pat Keriss
To: Dorling Kindersely books
Subject: Larry Grotter

I have devised a sure fire winner to plug a gap in the children's book market...

Introducing 'Larry Grotter'.

Larry is a 15 year old borstal boy who becomes embroiled in the drug scene in his home town of Widnes. He gets into a number of scrapes and always ends up getting 'nicked by the rozzers'.

Coming from a broken home, Larry can associate with a large number of the literate readership of this countries teen market...a market similar to your own.

There is always a moral to the story ending with Larry chanting.....'I'm Larry Grotter...don't F.C.U.K with drugs kids. Innit'.

I have discussed this idea with a number of voluntary groups and agencies in the South London area and they think it's great.

Would you like me to start writing ASAP?

Cheers

Pat Keriss

ps.....tell your 'literary staff on a Friday night' ...'don't F.C.U.K with cocaine. Innit'.

NO RESPONSE

108. Something for the wick end

From: Pat Keriss
To: Madame Tussauds
Subject: Wax

Hi,

I am running a CSE event in January (this stands for celebrity swinging event).

Basically this means that all those attending must come dressed up as a celebrity. They are then 'paired off' with the celebrity of a similar ilk. For example, I am coming as Paul McCartney. If for example a woman comes as a celebrity amputee (Heather mills, Kerrie off CBBC), then they will get paired off and so on.

I digress....from past events we have had feedback that the sexual enjoyment of our members (and their members) has been tainted by the lack of celebrity. Therefore I would like the next best thing.

Would you be willing to hire us the waxworks of Jordan, Michael Jackson, Steve McFadden and Amy Winehouse for the weekend event? I will ensure that any damage/ stains are wiped off prior to their return. I will even give a deposit should you so wish.

I have a friend with a transit van, so collection and delivery is no problemo.

Please could you tell me the likely cost?

As another gesture of goodwill, I would like to offer 2 tickets to staff at MT and also offer 2 tickets as a competition prize for guests.

Regards

Pat Keriss

NO RESPONSE

109. Taking the pistacchio

From: Pat Keriss
To: British Peanut council
Subject: Peanut world record

I am an advocate of peanuts and their virtues and have been for many a year.

To that end I have applied to Guinness for a peanut based world record. I currently hold a couple of world records, one for the most number of raisons a person has managed to get into their mouth and another for living in a horse box with a stallion called flakey (I held out for 16 days).

My peanut world record is crude to some but has gained press interest already. I aim to break the world record for the most peanuts 'insert-exit'. Basically using my mouth, ears and anus, I aim to hold in 750 peanuts for a period of 2 minutes without letting any out of my ears, anus and mouth. The current (unofficial) record is held by a peanut officianado from Holland who managed only 721. I aim to smash this by 29.

I would like to offer you a hoarding board, for free, as a backdrop to my attempt. This will be my way of thanking you for the wonderful peanuts you offer and will hopefully boost your readership.

I look forward to working with you.

Pat Keriss

NO RESPONSE

110. Rushdie

From: Pat Keriss
To: Salmon and trout association
Subject: Pungent

I loved Salmon...until a few days ago. Usually I grill my fish, but I decided the other day to cook it in the oven. I wish I hadn't and was sorely disappointed. The taste was akin to oral sex I had some years ago with an ex (hence why she is now an ex). It smelt pungent and made me retch (as did the Salmon the other night).

Is there any way to cook salmon in the oven but too also get rid of the pungent genital flavour that this form of cooking causes?

I would appreciate your advice.

NO RESPONSE

<u>111. Night time curlew</u>

From: Pat Keriss
To: Birddiary.co.uk
Subject: Slender billed curlews

Hello

I was recently in Russia and was amazed to see a group of 4 slender billed curlews.

Not sure why i'm telling you but thought you may be interested?

Pat Keriss

<u>NO RESPONSE</u>

112. Last post

From: Pat Keriss
To: Glen Stephens (stamp collector)
Subject: Stamp quote

Hi Glen

My lover (large age difference) recently left me a number of stamps in her will. To be honest, I haven't got a clue about stamps and was going to give them to charity but thought id see if you have any idea if there worth a few quid?

They are:
a british guiana 1c magenta and tre skilling banco yellow?

Thanks in advance

Pat

NO RESPONSE

113. Dentist chair

From: Pat Keriss
To: Yahoo news
Subject: Gaza

It is no wonder the footballer gaza has such a hard time and is battling alcohol and other addictions.

Why do you feel the need to run a story reporting 60 arrests over gaza protests? People have no reason to protest against gaza who, in the eyes of many, including myself, is a national hero and was a stalwart of the nearly victorious Euro 96 team.

All you will succeed in doing is putting this tortured genius into an early grave by running these stories. Maybe your time would be better spent extolling the virtues of Gaza (without mention to the wife beating) and less time reporting narrow minded and ignorant protests against him.

NO RESPONSE

114. You gander

From: Pat Keriss
To: Harvester
Subject: Harvester

I have a query regarding my son who works in one of your outlets...
My son is concerned as to what would happen to him with regard to a hypothetical question?
He is intellectually subadequate (formerly classed as remedial)...he has been working at Harvester for some year now. Anyhow, his manager bullies him. If he had (hypothetically) been, on a daily basis, masturbating on the chicken, urinating in the relish/ sauces, rubbing hot corn cobs on his genitalia, placing pubic hairs in the piri piri chicken sauce and wiping the bread rolls between his naked bum cheeks, what would happen to him if caught?
Idi Amin (Not real name)

NO RESPONSE

115. Twocking hell

From: Pat Keriss
To: Institute of advanced motorists
Subject: IAM membership

Hi,

I have recently been released from 12 years at her majesties pleasure for some serious offences (TWOC'ing, hit and run, burglary, driving at excessive speed (142mph), driving away from the scene of a crime, criminal damage and assault to name a few).

I have decided to right my wrongs and want to become an unlicensed cabbie to help provide for my 7 children.

What's the quickest and easiest way to join your club? Is there any way this process can be 'quickened' if you catch my drift?

Many thanks

Pat Keriss

From: IAM
To: Pat Keriss
Subject: IAM membership

I would ask you to go to our website www.iam.org.uk **and you will find everything you need to purchase one of our skill for life programmes or our fast track option there, the cost is £139 for the sfl prog, and £460 to do the fast track option .**
Graham Butler
Senior Administrative Assistant

From: Pat Keriss
To: IAM
Subject: IAM membership

That's great. Thanks.

So to clarify...you will pass me if I slip you £460? How would you like it? Im guessing cash...let me know where and ill get an associate to drop it off.

Cheers

Pat

From: IAM
To: Pat Keriss
Subject: IAM membership

The best way to purchase this is to go to our website www.iam.org.uk **if you go to search this site and put in fast track it will take you to the right page where you can apply for the fast track.**
Graham Butler
Senior Administrative Assistant

From: Pat Keriss
To: IAM
Subject: IAM membership

I am guessing from your avoiding my direct question that you are playing hardball in order to up the ante?

OK.....you win...ill bung you a bag of sand with a further monkey upon my getting the green light from the examiner.

I can't say fairer than that......

Pat

116. Transparent

From: Pat Keriss
To: Steel Window Association
Subject: Window quote

Hi,

Could you give me a quote for 12 medium sized wooden sash windows with drawstrings?

Regards

Pat

**From: Steel window association
To: Pat Keriss
Subject: Window quote**

Dear Pat

Apologies for the late response – I have been off sick.

The Steel Window Association has members who only work with steel windows, not wooden ones. I have attached our member's list so that you can contact any one of them for a quote on steel windows if you wish.

Regards

**Laura Lee
Steel Window Association**

From: Pat Keriss
To: Steel window association
Subject: Window quote

Dear Laura,

That must have been one heck of an illness? I sent the e mail 3 weeks ago. I trust you are now in good health?

I'm glad you responded...the property is getting damned cold now with the onset of Jack Frost and William Winter, yet my window problems still persist.

Do you not sell drawstring steel sash windows then? By not selling the wooden ones are you not limiting your market?

As my grandfather used to say 'Steel rusts...wood last for generations'. This is a mantra that I swear by and has held me in good stead (until recently).

Chin up and try a drop of lemon in some hot water at night. My Gran swore by it saying 'a lemon a day keeps the quack at bay'. This is another mantra by which I swear and has never done wrong by me.

I look forward to your response

Regards

Pat (Keriss)

From: Steel Window Association
To: Pat Keriss
Subject: Window quote

Dear Pat

Thank you very much for the advice, I am much better now.

I'm afraid that the SWA only has members who deal in steel windows, however some may also work with aluminium. I suggest you contact them individually from the attached list and perhaps see if they can advise you or tell you if they do sell drawstring steel sash windows.

We don't do any selling or have any products in this office as we simply run the secretariat for the Association.

Kind regards
Laura

Laura Lee
Steel Window Association

117. Wee Jimmy Krankie

From: Pat Keriss
To: Small landlords association
Subject: Small landlords

Hello

I would like to join the Small Landlords Association but am unsure if I fulfil the criteria?

I am 3'11 tall and classed as a 'terminal midget', NOT a hereditary or non hereditary dwarf....my parents however were both on the dwarf/ midget cusp.

Would my size allow me to enter the association? I have a bedsit in Herne Bay that I have let out to a man for the last few years.

Kind Regards

Pat Keriss

From: Small landlords association
To: Pat Keriss
Subject: small landlords

Dear Pat,
Thank you for your email, we are not the Small Landlords Association anymore we are the National Landlords Association. Are association is not based on the size of the landlord, but the properties they own.
You are more than welcome to join us, as long as you are a residential landlord. Please see our website for more details www.landlords.org.uk
Regards

Michelle Harris
Office Manager

From: Pat Keriss
To: Small landlords association
Subject: Small landlords

Dear Michelle

Thankyou for the reply. I must say I find the name of the association extremely misleading.

Are you saying that landlords must now own properties nationally to join the association, no matter what their height?

Many thanks

Pat Keriss

118. Rocket man

From: Pat Keriss
To: Sparks Cars
Subject: Firework scar

Do you just deal in cars? Or do you deal in scars made by sparks as I have been told?

I got hit in the face by a mini indoor firework some years ago and have a scar under my right eye. What advice would you give me regarding how to cover up the scar on a night out?

Pat Keriss

NO RESPONSE

119. Because

From: Pat Keriss
To: School of psychotherapy, Regents college
Subject: Thinking

I have two questions:

1) What am I thinking?
2) Why am I thinking what I am thinking?

Regards

Pat Keriss

NO RESPONSE

120. Turn in up to 11

From: Pat Keriss
To: Noise abatement society
Subject: Noisy neighbour

CAN YOU TELL ME WHAT TO DO IF I HAVE A NOISY NEIGHBOUR. THANKS. PAT KERISS

**From: Noise abatement society
To: Pat Keriss
Subject: Noisy neighbour**

Dear Pat

Please accept our sincere apologies for the delay in response to your email. A copy of our helpsheet on dealing with a noise complaint is now attached.

Do let us know how you get on, or contact us again if you feel we can help you further. The Noise Abatement Society is a registered charity, entirely dependent on voluntary donations to continue our work. Help us to maintain a service by making a donation or becoming a member via our website at www.noiseabatementsociety.com. All contributions are gratefully received.

<u>**Amanda Ogilvie**</u>

THE NOISE ABATEMENT SOCIETY

121. Pomp and ceremony

From: Pat Keriss
To: Portsmouth FC
Subject: Nwankwo Kanu puppet

Hi

I have been a long time Pompey fan. To that end, I have devised, produced and have been selling a football/ comedy item for the last few weeks with great results.

Introducing the 'Nwankwo Kanu puppet'.

Basically it has the likeness of Nwankwo but with a few differences. It has a phallus that when touched shouts 'nWANKwo'! After 18-20 strokes it screams 'Goooaaaallll'!

These have been going down a storm so far and I have sold hundreds. Would you like to buy some to sell in the club shop?

Play up Pompey!

Pat Keriss

NO RESPONSE

122. Pit pony

From: Pat Keriss
To: Aisma (Association of independence specialist medical accountants)
Subject: Aisma sufferer

Hello

I have suffered from quite serious aisma for a few years now. I get particularly out of breath and queasy after playing sports (rarely), walking up stairs (frequently) and enjoying sexual relations (daily).

Do you have any advice as to how to minimise the effects of undertaking physical exertion whilst suffering from aisma?

Many thanks

Pat Keriss

NO RESPONSE

123. Felling dogmatic

From: Pat Keriss
To: AITA (Adult industry trade association)
Subject: K9 Swings

My (underground) business is 'K9 Swings'. We arrange for private clients to have orgies/ swinging parties with dogs. Instead of car keys, the owners leave the leads in a bowl. Other owners choose a lead and they are then paired off with the dog whose lead they belong to.

The members do not hurt anybody. If I join your association, would you fight shoulder to shoulder to legalise K9 parties and take it from its underground lair?

Many thanks

NO RESPONSE

124. Julio

From: Pat Keriss
To: ARCA (Asbestos removal contractors association)
Subject: Blue asbestos

I would like some advice if possible.... a couple of weeks ago I removed some asbestos from the loft (it is a safe type apparently called 'blue' asbestos). Anyhow, I have tried to have someone remove this since I slipped a disc a couple of weeks ago. Everyone is refusing. I currently have it sitting in my twins room and would like it moved as they don't have enough room to run around and they are grouchy due to both having coughs. Do you know anyone who could pop around in the next couple of weeks to clear this mess from their bedroom?

Thanks

From: ARCA
To: Pat Keriss
Subject: Blue asbestos

Dear Pat
Thank you for your email.
Please could you call me on 01283 531126 to discuss this matter further.

Yours sincerely

Geoff Silver
BSc MBA PGCE MIfL CMIOSH
Membership Compliance Manager

From: Pat Keriss
To: ARCA
Subject: Blue asbestos

Dear Geoff
Thanks for the reply. Sorry, but I work all day, do not have a mobile phone and am not allowed off the production line to make personal phone calls. Do you know anyone who could come and shift this mess? Many thanks, Pat

125. Eartha Kitt

From: Pat Keriss
To: NHS Direct
Subject: Cockney pain

I've got some gip with my hampton. I kipped behind the back of my duchess of Fyfe with a one time looker. I now feel uncle dick and my Niagara falls are in a right two and eight. I've scrubbed it for tony benn days with some cape of good hope with no joy.

My hampton also hurts when i take a mickey bliss which makes me want to pipe my eye and has left me laid up in my uncle ned.

Her indoors wont let me near the berkshire hunt or fryar tuck her khybur pass. All she will do is fiddle with my outings and festivals and cum on her north and south or derby kelly.

It hurts. Please help

NO RESPONSE

126. Kerb crawler

From: Pat Keriss
To: LTDA (Licensed Taxi driver association)
Subject: Taxi advice

Hi,

I would like some advice....

I am an unlicensed cabbie with many years experience around the UK. I have just moved to London and wondered where the best places were to pick up fares from the street?

I provide a cheap, fast service but I need to improve my income as I am in debt and haven't been able to afford basics such as a service and insurance for the last 8 months.

I really would appreciate your help.

Cheers

Pat

NO RESPONSE

127. Au Natural

From: Pat Keriss
To: The ramblers association
Subject: Naked rambling

I was interested to read about your 'winter walks'. As a nudist of many years standing I am extremely hardy as are some of my (male friends). There are a group of 5 of us from Newbury. We call ourselves the 'Nudebury ramblers'...you may have heard of us?

Anyhow, we would like join your association and walk naked on a number of your winter walks. We would also like to ask (through your website) your members to join us in enjoying the crisp winter as nature intended....au natural.

I trust we can look forward to your support and we look forward to meeting you on a number of your walks soon.

Pat Keriss

NO RESPONSE

128. Dennis

From: Pat Keriss
To: Anglian Potters society
Subject: Anglian potters

Hi,

I am after a unique birthday present for my father who is from Anglia. His name is David Potter. I am sure he would enjoy being part of the Anglian Potters society and getting to meet other Potters locally. He has been into his family tree research thing for quite a while.

Please could you tell me how much it would be for the gold/top rate membership and how many members of the potter family you are in contact with?

Many thanks

Pat

NO RESPONSE

129. Billy big bullocks

From: Pat Keriss
To: BBC Question time
Subject: Dimbleby

I was concerned to read Mr Dimbleby could not present question time due to a problem with one of his Bollocks.

I too have had a problem with one of my bollocks after an extremely hot holiday and the wearing of unsuitable clothing around the genital region.

This was cleared up following a GP visit. I would suggest Mr Dimbleby does similarly.

Yours

Pat Keriss

NO RESPONSE

130. Hairy strikers

From: Pat Keriss
To: thefoodguruonline.co.uk
Subject: Food demonstrations

I am confused? With the rise in this countries obesity levels, why don't supermarkets stop selling buy one get one free offers? To get to the stage where companies such as yours have to go into stores and openly demonstrate against food is shocking.

Good luck with the demos however and I have plenty of wood and paint should you wish me to produce some boards to hold at your demonstrations.

Power to the people!

Pat

From: thefoodgugonline.co.uk
To: Pat Keriss
Subject: Food demonstrations

Your email makes no sense and holds no valid argument against the work I do..............

Regards,
The Food Guru

From: Pat Keriss
To: thefoodguruonline.co.uk
Subject: Food demonstrations

I am confused?

Don't you demonstrate against food and food suppliers?

Regards

Pat

**From: thefoodguruonline.co.uk
To: Pat Keriss
Subject: Food demonstrations**

**Nooooo!! I demonstrate foods and cooking equipment!
Recipes to encourage people to cook and enjoy food!**

**Regards,
Rob Fletcher**

From: Pat Keriss
To: thefoodguruonline.co.uk
Subject: Food demonstrations

Then you should re-name what you do!

It is due to Charlatans like you that we are obese and staring into the trough shaped abyss. Shame on you!

I myself weigh 26 stone due to the marketing of buy one get one free deals and discounted food offers. This is solely down to the supermarkets and scoundrels like yourself.

Pat

**From: thefoodguruonline.co.uk
To: Pat Keriss
Subject: Food demonstrations**

**You weigh 26 stone due to your lack of will power and laziness when it comes to preparing fresh food and ingredients. Get real cherish this.............. Your last reply from me!!
Regards,
The Food Guru**

131. AM/ FM

From: Pat Keriss
To: The British Audio visual dealers association
Subject: blaupunkt, kenwood etc....

Hi

I have a number of second hand car home surround sound systems for sale. I have around 40 blaupunkt, sony, kenwood and alba systems at very low prices with no questions asked. I will only take cash though, so make me an offer.

Ta

Pat

NO RESPONSE

132. Tool

From: Pat Keriss
To: Gyles Brandreth management
Subject: Gyles Brandreth

Hi Mandy

I work freelance for a few TV production companies and was wondering if one of your clients, Gyles Brandreth, might be interested in a little talking head piece to camera on a show we are working on?

It is provisionally entitled 'length' and it about minor celebrities in the public eye who are classed as being a 'length/ penis' by the public at large.

It will not be a hatchet job, but merely a study as to why these 'celebs' believe the public find them irksome and whether or not this is a carefully cultivated image or not?

I would appreciate a positive reply as we are a little overloaded at present with former reality TV stars.

regards

Pat

NO RESPONSE

133. Smokey and the bandit

From: Pat Keriss
To: British Record dealers association
Subject: Howard Marks

Could you tell me who the biggest selling UK dealer is of all time? My friend thinks it's Howard Marks after importing around 100 tons of Dope into the UK. I've got £20 on it saying its not.

Many Thanks

Pat

NO RESPONSE

<u>134. 5-3?</u>

From: Pat Keriss
To: British Aggregates association
Subject: Barnet v Stevenage

Can you tell me the aggregate score between Barnet and Stevenage in the Herts Senior cup semi final from 1997?

I have searched archives everywhere and you are my last hope.

Keep up the good work.

Pat

NO RESPONSE

135. Big dope

From: Pat Keriss
To: The British Gear association (Engineering gear company)
Subject: Gear enquiry

If, hypothetically, someone found a Kilo of high grade gear (i.e. charris) on the coastline whilst on a walk, what would the approximate street value be?

Many thanks

Pat

NO RESPONSE

136. Albert

From: Pat Keriss
To: British Herb Trading association
Subject: Herb trading

Hi Tim

I have been left a small inheritance of around 5 grand. Having just finished college and still having lots of contacts within seats of learning across London, I am looking for a partner in my new Herb Trading venture.

I can't think of anyone better to be able to trade high grade 'erb in the London area.

Can I ask what percentage you would like and what contacts you can bring to the party?

Peace out.

Pat

NO RESPONSE

137. Slippery

From: Pat Keriss
To: The UK lubricants association
Subject: LUBE magazine

I recently came across (excuse the pun) your LUBE magazine.

Being a sexually permissive man in is 50's with plenty of m/f, m/m, m/m/f, m/f/f and m/m/f/f/f/ts experience I was hoping to submit an article for publication?

It would be a thought provoking trip down memory lane with a number of lube related stories and anecdotes.

Please can you give me a word count? Also can I name specific brands by name?

Keep up the good work.

Pat

NO RESPONSE

138. Sleazy listening

From: Pat Keriss
To: British Phonographic Industry (BPI)
Subject: Home made video

Please can you tell me the best way to have a home made pornographic film of me and my married friends distributed abroad including to Amsterdam?

We believe that our video is unique and our no holds barred narcotics fuelled romps would be a hit in the European sleaze capital, as they are a little too racy for the UK domestic market.

Many thanks

Pat Keriss

NO RESPONSE

139. Headroom

From: Pat Keriss
To: Max Clifford
Subject: Prince of pictures

Hi Max

Hypothetically, if someone had a series of 5 high quality, colour pictures of a well known prince snorting and smoking illegal narcotics whilst wearing only a pair of y fronts and a ladies wig at a private party, what would they fetch on the open market?

Many thanks

Pat

NO RESPONSE

140. Stitch up

From: Pat Keriss
To: Machine knitting monthly magazine
Subject: world record Knit?

Firstly thankyou! My grandmother is 99 and an avid reader of Machine Knitting Monthly. Her knitting has given her a new lease of life since she lost her legs and a kidney a few years ago in an unfortunate accident in her Lebanese made stairlift.

Anyhow, after a long period of depression, she took to knitting again and has been working for 12 years on her piece d'resistance....the 'Knit wit'. This is an amusing comedy character I devised in my spare time for use by the TV people. As yet I have still to find a suitable vehicle for 'Knit wit' and his zany wool based capers.

My grandmother however has shown unnerving faith and has knitted a 3D Knit wit measuring 18 feet tall (out of her woollen stilettos).

I am wondering, is this a world record for a knitted character?

Keep up the good work!

Pat Keriss

From: Machine knitting monthly
To: Pat Keriss
Subject: World record knit

Hi Pat

Thanks so much for writing and I'm catching up with a full in-box. I'd love to feature this in the magazine and wonder if you have a picture of the knitting - and also one of your grandmother? It's a lovely story and it would have much more impact with a photograph or two. Could you also let me have your grandmother's name and address, although only her name (or first name if she prefers) will appear in the magazine. Best wishes from Anne
Publisher & Editor - Machine Knitting Monthly

From: Pat Keriss
To: Machine knitting monthly
Subject: World record knit

Hi Ann

That's wonderful news! I informed grandmother who has been a little obstinate and has been 'knit picking' me about the e mail you set all weekend (excuse the pun!).

Anyhow, she agreed to be photographed which you will be glad of. However we did encounter a problem....the problem is that the 'Knit wit' is now so large it is stored in my brother's garage. Mother has been working on various body parts which she then knits on once we spend a couple of hours loading the 'Knit wit' into the back of an open bed trailer then carefully manoeuvring it into her house (whilst trying not to damage too many items...at the last count we have only broken 2 vases and a door handle).
I digress...We took a picture of the 'Knit wit' and one of my mother which I then gave to a friend who is adept in the use of 'foto-shop?'. They have superimaged the pictures together (sorry...all a little too technical for me). I have attached the picture; I just hope it is of sufficient quality to print? She will be made up if it is.

Her name is Ruby Heek-Cegg. She lives in Barnet, Hertfordshire.
I look forward to your response.
Pat

From: Machine knitting monthly
To: Pat Keriss
Subject: World record knit

Hi Pat
 Wow - this is absolutely fabulous and I'm sure I can fit it into the February 2010 magazine. Please thank your grandmother and congratulate her from all of us on her amazing achievement. Very well done Ruby! I'll combine your letters carefully, so the readers know what it's all about and thanks, once again, for telling us all about it.
Best wishes from Anne

141. Plastic fantastic

From: Pat Keriss
To: www.makingcardsmagazine.co.uk
Date: Thursday 19th November 2009
Subject: plastic cards

Hi Liz

Do you sell blank plastic Master/ Visa cards?

I need some for an amdram production of 'Wall Street'.

How much would 10,000 blanks cost?

Many Thanks

Pat

From: www.makingcardsmagazine.co.uk
To: Pat Keriss
Subject: Plastic cards

Dear Pat,

I'm afraid we do not sell Visa cards, we only sell magazines and patterned papers.

Regards

Liz

From: Pat Keriss
To: www.makingcardsmagazine.co.uk
Subject: Plastic cards

Hi Liz,

When you say patterned paper...do you mean 'driving licences'?

I can pay top dollar.....
 Pat

142. House of horrors

From: Pat Keriss
To: Metal Hammer magazine
Subject: Metal hammer

A very confusing website you have there....

I am looking to purchase a Featherlite Deluge Titanium hammer.

I understand it won't be cheap, but can you quote me for 2 of them?

Many thanks

Pat

From: (James Gill) Metal hammer magazine
To: Pat Keriss
Subject: Metal hammer

http://www.gareth.com/Vaughan-07170-14-Ounce-Titanium-Straight/dp/B000H6W8TS

From: Pat Keriss
To: Metal Hammer magazine
Subject: Metal hammer

Dear Gill

Thanks for the response.

I think you have misunderstood. Although happy with the 14 oz Daluge titanium, I am none too impressed with the Hickory handle. Do you have any with oak/ teak handles? Also, I want discount for two.

Thanks

Pat Keriss

143. No positives

From: Pat Keriss
To: Scots Magazine
Subject: Scot can I do?

Hi, I am hoping you can assist me?

I am a University student. I have recently been given my toughest assignment yet. The assignment is entitled 'turning a stereotype on its head' and I have been given the topic based on 'Scotland'.

With your dire football team, unattractive females, shocking weather, violent language, dreadful music and dress sense and lack of social skills and community cohesion, I am struggling for copy.

If you could point me in the direction of one (even mildly) positive thing about being a Scot I would appreciate it.

I know it's a big ask, but here's hoping.....

och aye fae noo.

Pat Keriss

NO RESPONSE

144. Scraping the misery barrel

From: Pat Keriss
To: Scots gay magazine
Subject: Frolics

Hi

I belong to a local Barnet based gay group called 'Bargay'.

We are a new group interested in socialising, swinging and George Michael basically!

We are all very middle class and would like to meet some bits of rough/ common gay people from around the UK. Obviously when we thought of common, someone mentioned that maybe we could invite some of yours Scots gays down for a weekend of frolics with no questions asked.

We don't have many blue collar workers down here and would welcome the hard working, uneducated Scots gay contingent with open arms.

Is this something your friends/ readers would be interested in, maybe in early January?

We can accommodate and pay travel should travel costs be an issue.

Many thanks

Pat

From: Scots gay magazine
To: Pat Keriss
Subject: Frolics

Hi Pat

Thank you for your email, I have placed below our latest ScotsGay Magazine display advert offers information as you may wish to advertise with us.
Let me know your thoughts. Jean Genie

To: Scots Gay magazine
From: Pat Keriss
Subject: Frolics

Dear 'Jean',

Are you the Jean Genie of the song?

If so, is it true that you live on your back and love chimney stacks?

In anticipation,

Pat

145. Pleasurable yank

From: Pat Keriss
To: Swing (over 50's lifestyle) magazine
Subject: Americano

Hi Sherry

By chance I have just cum across your magazine and my eyes lit up.

I am a 28 year old male in the UK who is interested in swinging with over 50 year old Americans (of both sexes).

Do you have a few contact names and numbers of such readers so I can set the wheels in motion? I have a thing for rough sex and grey hair. Having an American accent is the cherry on this particular pie and I can't wait for your reply.

Keep up the good work sexy cheeks

Pat

x

NO RESPONSE

146. Griffin

From: Pat Keriss
To: Weightwatchers magazine
Subject: Magazine sponsorship

Hello

I am the UK press officer for a famous British National political party. We feel that out aims and ethos fit perfectly with the message weighwatchers put across and we would like to sponsor the magazine (and appear on all the front covers). 'Weightwatchers magazine....sponsored by...' type of thing.

Is this something you would consider? if so, what is the likely cost?

Regards

Pat Keriss

NO RESPONSE

147. Uphill gardener

From: Pat Keriss
To: Brighton and Hove council
Subject: Gaybi allotment

In the name of equality, I would like to set up a 'gay-bi' allotment in the Brighton area. Having faced prejudice around the Sussex region for simply walking my dog late at night in parkland, I, along with my friends, believe that an allotment where we could shovel in the day and meet and walk our dogs at night in privacy would be a great fillip to the gay and bi male population of Brighton. We would police the site fully and would insist on the erection of a gate and buzzer entry to prevent undesirables from unauthorized entry.

We feel that giving somewhere peaceful at night to our community to discuss gardening and meet socially would be great for the gaybi community.

From: Brighton and Hove council
To: Pat Keriss
Subject: Gaybi allotment

Dear Pat
You are able to apply for an allotment plot by going online at http://www.brighton-hove.gov.uk/index.cfm?request=c1200934
I will forward you comments to the Countryside Access Manager who is responsible for the allotments.
Kind regards
Fiona Cyster
Senior Administrator
Cityparks

From: Pat Keriss
To: Brighton and Hove council
Subject: Gaybi allotment

Dear Fiona

You're sidestepping of my queries and lack of coherent answers to my specific questions render me speechless and somewhat perturbed.

Do you not agree that a Gaybi allotment would be a good thing for the Gay, Bi and Trans (pre and post op) community?

It strikes me that the council are a bunch of homophobes. Don't you agree?

Shame on you all. Up the pink movement!

Pat

From: Brighton and Hove Council
To: Pat Keriss
Subject: Gaybi allotment

Dear Pat Keriss
The council operates an inclusive allotment service and applications for allotments are welcome from all residents of the city. If you have experienced prejudice anywhere in the city, including allotments and parks, please contact us and/or the Police with details as appropriate.
However please note allotments are not appropriate places for exercising dogs.

If you are unhappy with my reply please do not hesitate to contact me and I will try and resolve any outstanding issues. Alternatively, you can contact the Standards and Complaints Team. You should write to them stating why you are not happy with the reply you have received and what you would like the council to do to put things right. The address to write to is Brighton and Hove City Council Standards and Complaints Team FREEPOST SEA2560 BRIGHTON BN1 1ZW or by email to complaints@brighton-hove.gov.uk,Fiona Cyster

148. d.i.v.o.r.c.e

From: Pat Keriss
To: www.weddingmagazine.co.uk
Subject: Divorce competitions

I control the budget for a large firm of solicitors who specialise in divorce law. We would like to run a series of sponsorships and high profile adverts in your magazine. We would also like to offer prizes such as '10 free divorces to be won' to interested parties. Please can you tell me the likely ball park figure of such an undertaking?
Regards

From: www.weddingmagazine.co.uk
To: Pat Keriss
Subject: Divorce competitions

I am sorry. This is not something we would be interested in. We are a wedding magazine. Not a divorce magazine.

From: Pat Keriss
To: www.weddingmagazine.co.uk
Subject: Divorce competitions

Hello

With the divorce rate at 11.9 couples per 1000 per year, I would have thought that this would be another string to your bow. I am sure that a number of people having clandestine affairs who are already married would appreciate the opportunity to get a free divorce.

This is something you should encourage your unhappy readers to partake in as opposed to putting on the blinkers and saying you will get married and live happily ever after. Sadly life isn't like that. I should know, I am now on wife number 4.

You will increase your advertising revenue and receive some cracking prizes to boot.

I look forward to your re-consideration.
Pat

From: www.weddingmagazine.co.uk
To: Pat Keriss
Subject: Divorce competitions

Dear Pat,

I'm afraid this really isn't something for our magazine as it is purely wedding-orientated, but if you would prefer to contact our publisher, his name is Roger Cummings roger_cummings@ipcmedia.com.

Many thanks,

Roshina

From: Pat Keriss
To: www.weddingmagazine.co.uk
Subject: Divorce competitions

Dear Roshina

Is this a joke? Cummings as in husbands and wife's cummings and goings?

Divorce is a serious business. It brings joy to millions of unhappily trapped people around the world on a daily basis.

I'll be goings now then.

Most amusing I don't think.

Pat

149. Taking it up the glitter

From: Pat Keriss
To: Quintessentially magazine (High brow lifestyle magazine/ private club)
Subject: Client

Good evening

I represent a huge internationally renowned recording artist.

He is interested in your services but is curious as to other members? He basically wants to enquire as to the quality of company he will be keeping if he joins?

I would appreciate a prompt response as he is due in London next week.

Many thanks

Pat

**From: Quintessentially magazine (High brow lifestyle magazine/ private club)
To: Pat Keriss
Subject: Client**

Thank you for your email Pat,

Our members range from entrepreneurs, A list celebrities, Royalty, high net worth business men and women from around the globe all in the forbes rich list. Please understand that we cannot provide any names due to confidentiality.

I would be happy to discuss this in more depth and email you some more information about Quintessentially.

**Please could you also provide me with your full daytime contact telephone number. I shall look forward to your reply.
My Kindest regards
David Zarzecki, Regional Sales Director, Quintessentially**

From: Pat Keriss
To: Quintessentially magazine (High brow lifestyle magazine/ private club)
Subject: Client

Dear David,

Thankyou for the response. I understand your need for confidentiality. I trust you understand my position also.

If you could send some more information via e mail, I will discuss it with Paul when I meet him on Wednesday.

Regards

Pat

From: Quintessentially magazine (High brow lifestyle magazine/ private club)
To: Pat Keriss
Subject: Client

Dear Pat,

Thank you for expressing an interest in a Quintessentially membership. We'd be only too happy to answer any questions you may have about our service but, in the meantime, please find some additional information on Quintessentially below.
With an unrivalled global reach, we have offices in Casablanca, Copenhagen, Dubai, Dublin, Geneva, Hong Kong, Istanbul, Jeddah, Johannesburg, Kuwait, London, Los Angeles, Maputo, Mexico City, Miami, Milan, Moscow, New York, Oslo , Panama, Paris, Rome, San Francisco, Seoul, Shanghai, Singapore, Stockholm, Sydney, Tokyo, Valletta, Vienna.
Quintessentially has quickly become an essential part of our members' lives, Quintessentially not only solves some of most pressing dilemmas (where to find presents in a hurry, a good nanny, the best gym in town) and saves you money but we can also help you make the most of your spare time.

We can get you into the best restaurants, health clubs, concerts, plays, operas, sporting events and exclusive nightclubs.

From last minute travel arrangements to impossible-to-find tickets, Quintessentially can almost certainly organise any kind of request – major or minor.
Quintessentially are committed to providing excellent service. Whether it's travel, music, art, restaurants, hotels, clubs, gyms, restaurants - we aim to bring you nothing but the best.

Kind regards,

David Zarzecki
Regional Sales Director
Quintessentially

From: Pat Keriss
To: Quintessentially magazine (High brow lifestyle magazine/ private club)
Subject: Client

Dear David,

It certainly makes interesting reading.

My client has decided he would like to join Qunitessentially. In return you will also receive the Kudos of the membership of a luminary in the field of popular music.

My clients (real) name is Paul Gadd.

Please can you forward me the relevant documentation for his perusal?

Regards

Pat

From: Quintessentially magazine (High brow lifestyle magazine/ private club)
To: Pat Keriss
Subject: Client

Thank you for your email Pat.

Please can I confirm that your client is Paul Gadd (Garry Glitter), this will be submitted to our membership committee for review.

My Kindest regards

David

David Zarzecki
Regional Sales Director
Quintessentially

From: Pat Keriss
To: Quintessentially magazine (High brow lifestyle magazine/ private club)
Subject: Client

Yes. That is affirmative.

I look forward to a positive reply as does Mr Gadd.

Is it possible to have temporary membership in the meantime?

Regards

Pat

150. Felix

From: Pat Keriss
To: Cat world magazine
Subject: Cat video

Hello

I recently returned from a trip to China. I was surprised at the widespread eating of cats as a form of nourishment. Anyhow, I am attempting to forge a career in the media and I have an interesting proposition for you.....

I have constructed a short 10 minute video in which I present and star with graphic footage of cats being cooked and eaten. My proposal is therefore beneficial to us both:

I provide you with a great video for your website homepage showing your viewers the dangers of eating cat meat, and I in turn get a welcome boost to my fledgling media career.

I look forward to your response.

Pat

NO RESPONSE

151. Grus 2

From: Pat Keriss
To: Cranes Today magazine
Subject: Crane wingspan

I am confused as to the pictures of buildings on your website?

Basically I am a huge fan of cranes (Grus Grus) and I have a query....

What is the largest wingspan ever recorded for a UK based crane?

Many thanks

From: Cranes Today magazine
To: Pat Keriss
Subject: Crane wingspan

Hi Pat,

Thanks for the interest. I'm afraid we just deal with the metal type of crane, not the ones with feathers.

Regards,

Will North

152. Arf Arf

From: Pat Keriss
To: RSPB
Subject: Aggressive chuffs

I live in Hampstead and I have a number of aggressive chuffs infiltrating my back yard. What is the best way to get rid of aggressive chuffs that seems intent on raking dirt up in my back alley?

many thanks

NO RESPONSE

153. Cull em' Jamie

From: Pat Keriss
To: Jazzmagazine.com
Subject: Jazzjazz magazine

Hi Jon,

Firstly may I say that I love Jazz from what I know of it.

Secondly, I have a proposition for you....

I am interested in the female (nude) form and have a healthy red blooded collection of what I term as 'Jazz mags'. Tonight I decided to look at some fresh websites and inadvertently came across your site (not literally you'll be glad to hear!).

Anyhow, I was surprised by the abundance of female beauty within your pages (Diana Krall and Lizz Wright to name but two stunners). With this in mind I got thinking.....I am a semi pro photographer. I would like to produce a one off magazine celebrating the female Jazz artist form and call it the 'Jazzjazz magazine'. This will be aimed at the high end perusers of soft pornography/ the female nude form.

I would appreciate it if you could pass me the contact telephone numbers for Diana, Lizz and any other Jazzy females you are acquainted with? In return I will send you some copies and give you a 'thanks' on the inside cover.

I look forward to your reply and to working with you in the near future.

Pat

NO RESPONSE

154. R Tards

From: Pat Keriss
To: Southwark Council
Subject: Community warden

Hi,

I am desperate for a job and was hoping you could help me?

My skill set is that I am a complete retard with an extremely basic mastery of the English language, no customer service skills, intellect or qualifications.

I enjoy wearing red jackets and a name badge in order to highlight my 'importance'. I have an aggressive demeanour and no decipherable talent.

With my skill set in mind, I think Id be perfect as a Southwark community warden. Can you e mail me an application pack?

Pat Keriss

From: Southwark Council
To: Pat Keriss
Subject: Community warden

Dear Pat Keriss,

Thank you for your email. I have forwarded your enquiry to the Jobs Help services, who will respond to your enquiry.

Please do not hesitate to contact us should you require any further assistance.

Yours Sincerely

Customer Service Centre
csc@southwark.gov.uk

From: Southwark Council
To: Pat Keriss
Subject: Community warden

Dear Pat,
Thank you very much for your email and expressing your interest in working with Southwark. All jobs within Southwark are advertised on your recruitment website www.jobsatsouthwark.gov.uk Candidates can view adverts and apply directly for the roles that we have on offer.
Once again, thank you for your interest.

Paula King

155. Painters in

From: Pat Keriss
To: Period Ideas (Interior design magazine)
Subject: Period remedies

Hi Daniel

Some one passed me your e mail address after I told them about some remedies I find help me with my period.

Once I get that first bloated feeling every month, I mix a glass of hot water with some ground pepper and lemon juice. It works wonders with my tummy ache and doesn't make me so cranky!

Another trick I use is to do 12 stomach crunches and then pass a large, firm stool. Again this relieves pressure and relieves the flow once I come on.

I hope this helps and you are able to publish my tips in your magazine.

Pat

NO RESPONSE

156. Big Tissue

From: Pat Keriss
To: Big Issue
Subject: Moral Dilemma

Please inform me as to the street etiquette regarding the following dilemma:

One of your vendors had one copy of the big issue left. I arrived at the point of sale at the same time as another paying punter. The vendor took money from us both and then gave his last copy to the other punter. The vendor informed me that he had now 'sold out' and offered 'no refunds'.

Clearly riled, I asked if he had heard of the term 'beggars can't be choosers' at which juncture he set his Jack Russell about me causing minor lacerations to my left shin.

I shant be purchasing your publication again.

Pat Keriss

From: Big issue magazine
To: Pat Keriss
Subject: Moral dilemma

Pat,

I am very sorry to hear about this incident, which must have been very distressing.

The vendor clearly fleeced you for money, and then attacked you. Can you let me know where this happened, and if you have any information that may help us identify the vendor so we can stop him from selling.

Would you like me to send you a copy of this week's issue in lieu of the copy you were refused?

Regards

Paul Joseph

From: Pat Keriss
To: Big issue magazine
Subject: Moral dilemma

Paul,

Yes...it was distressing, but thankyou for your concern anyhow.

It happened in East London and the vendor had a beard, matted hair and a string on which he kept his dog. Hopefully that should help you to apprehend him ASAP.

I'm ok for the copy thankyou. Think I'll stick to Homes and Gardens magazine from here on in...It's safer!

Pat

157. Pinhead

From: Pat Keriss
To: British Acupuncture council
Subject: The needle

Last summer I had some acupuncture from someone who claimed to be fully qualified. Anyhow, I have had serious head and chest pains since which I believed was due to the 200 or so needles I had put into me to cure a number of ailments including dizziness, fatigue, migraines, vertigo and an over active thyroid.

I recently went through customs on my way to a stamp collector's convention in Idaho. Inadvertently I set of the security alarm and, to cut a long story short, had to undergo the indignity of a strip search. With the alarm still going off I was refused passage and ended up having to watch the convention on webcam.

I believe the acupuncture(er) left a number of needles in my head and chest. The pain is immense and to be blunt I would like to know what the bloody hell you intend to do about it?

Pat Keriss

From: British Acupuncture council
To: Pat Keriss
Subject: The needle

Dear Pat Keriss

Your e-mail has been passed to me for comment.

First, while the BAcC is the largest body of professional acupuncturists in the UK, acupuncture is not a statutorily regulated activity, and we do not have jurisdiction over everyone practising or claiming to be qualified. There are several other associations which have practising members, as well as about 10,000 medical practitioners using acupuncture regularly.

If the person who gave you treatment is one of our members we would take this very seriously indeed, and if you can provide us with the name of the practitioner concerned we can check whether this is the case. If they do not belong to the BAcC, they may belong to another professional body whom you may need to contact as soon as possible. If they do not belong to a professional association, you may be able to seek redress through your local Trading Standards Office or the local authority Enviromental Health Department who register acupuncturists wherever they work.

Second, if you suspect that the alarms were set off by a retained acupuncture needle or needles, you need to visit your GP as a matter of urgency and have this checked by X-ray. BAcC members are thoroughly trained to ensure that they do not leave needles in patients and would be severely dealt with if they did. They also do not use what are termed 'retained needles', where the needles are left in place for several days and taped down. However, some practitioners of other associations may use this technique.

On the basis of what you say I suspect it is highly unlikely that the practitoner belongs to the BAcC because the number of needles involved would be far beyond what we would expect someone to be using. However, as I said earlier, if you are happy to provide us with information on who gave you the treatment we can take further steps if that person falls within our jurisdiction or direct you to the appropriate organisations to seek redress.

I hope this provides you with sufficient information to pursue the matter to your satisfaction.

Yours sincerely

John Wheeler
Secretary

158. Jules Rimet

From: Pat Keriss
To: Northern Irish FA
Subject: The weald cup

I am currently arranging an 'alternative' world cup for those teams unlucky not to make it to South Africa. After your close defeat to France in the play off's, I would like to invite you to a 4 team 'weald cup' to be played at Wealdstone's ground. The other teams in this competitive competition will be yourselves, Rayners Lane and Tooting and Mitchum United.

We have player's spare rooms that your players can sleep in during the month long tournament and we are looking to gain an exclusive TV package from the renowned BCTV (Barnet community television).

Please confirm that you will be able to attend?

Regards

From: Northern Irish FA
To: Pat Keriss
Subject: The weald cup

Hi Pat

With regards to your email I would just like to inform you that you are
through to the wrong FA, we are the Irish Football Association of
NORTHERN IRELAND, you should be contacting the Football Association of
IRELAND, contact number is 003531 8999500 or website address is
www.fai.ie

Kind Regards

Angela McKibbin
Marketing Department
Irish Football Association

From: Pat Keriss
To: Northern Irish FA
Subject: The weald cup

Hi Angela,

Really? I'm sorry.

I'll look out for you at the world cup. Who have you got in round 1?

All the best

Pat

From: Northern Irish FA
To: Pat Keriss
Subject: The Weald cup

Hi Pat

You are ok, unfortunately we didn't make it through to the World Cup, we finished 4th in our group, Slovakia and Slovenia finished top of our group, maybe the next World Cup we will qualify.

Kind Regards

Angela McKibbin
Marketing Department
Irish Football Association

From: Pat Keriss
To: Northern Irish FA
Subject: The Weald cup

Dear Angela

I hope so. That is a shame.

With that in mind, do you think your team would be able to play in the 'weald cup' as I outlined in a previous e mail?
Many thanks. Pat

From: Northern Irish FA
To: Pat Keriss
Subject: The Weald cup

Hi Pat

I know, well hopefully we will be able to qualify for the next World Cup, don't see why not!

Best Wishes

Angela McKibbin
Marketing Department
Irish Football Association

From: Pat Keriss
To: Northern Irish FA
Subject: The Weald cup

Hi Angela

No reason why not...my friend says you have one of the best centre fronts in the world in Robbie Keen.

I will follow your progress with vigour and gusto.

Pat

From: Northern Irish FA
To: Pat Keriss
Subject: The weald cup

Hi Pat

You're friend is giving you the wrong information, Robbie Keane plays for Ireland, our centre forwards are David Healy, Warren Feeney, Kyle Lafferty and Martin Paterson.

Best Wishes
Angela McKibbin
Marketing Department
Irish Football Association

From: Pat Keriss
To: Northern Irish FA
Subject: The weald cup

Hi Angela,

I'm sorry...I must be getting a little muddled. Usually my football knowledge is superb.

I am a little confused by David Healy's name however...isn't that the old Labour politician with the bushy monobrow? I would have thought he would be a bit aged to play international football now?

Pat

From: Northern Irish FA
To: Pat Keriss
Subject: The weald cup

Hi Pat

Oh I wouldn't worry about it, you're not the only one!

David Healy is 34 and from Killyleagh, we was the leading goalscorer in the World Cup 2006 Qualifiers, beating Davor Zuker!!

Best Wishes

Angela McKibbin
Marketing Department
Irish Football Association

159. Boreham

From: Pat Keriss
To: Littlewoods
Subject: Little woods

Hi,

I was wondering what the office consensus is for your favourite little wood?

I really enjoy ambling weekend walks through wooded luminaries such as Keg Wood, Coghurst Wood, Woodcock Wood, Sawmill wood, Binsey wood, Odens wood and sparrowhawks wood.

What are your favourite little woods?

Many thanks

Pat

From: Littlewoods
To: Pat Keriss
Subject: Little woods

Dear Customer

Thanks for your email about your enquiry.
Unfortunately i feel you have got our site mixed up with another site. Littlewoods Europe is a online shopping website. We do not have any information about walking weekends through wooded illuminaries.

If you have any further questions, just let me know - I'll be happy to help you.

Kind Regards
Richard Morton
Online Customer Care

160. Persian

From: Pat Keriss
To: trugmakers.co.uk
Subject: T rug

Hi Kevin

I am really interested in getting one of your 'T' shaped rugs for my new house.

My husband's name is Trevor and it would be a great housewarming present for him.

I would like an 8x10 foot rug made from the finest Moreno wool to place in from of the log fire.

Please can you quote me a price?

Many thanks

Pat

From:Trugmakers.co.uk
To: Pat Keriss
Subject: T rug

Hi,
I make TRUGS not T Rugs!!!! Please click here www.trugmakers.co.uk
Regards
Kevin

161. Environ mental

From: Pat Keriss
To: Woodlands.co.uk
Subject: Help

Hi Simon

I'm hoping you can point me in the right direction....?

I would like to 'use/ borrow' a secluded wood. To cut a long story short (and between you and me) I am interested in somewhere hidden to dispose of a series of drums, some leaking, containing thousands of gallons of used engine oil.

I have a JCB digger so would be able to rip up a few acres of trees and bury the evidence pretty quickly. The lead time should be around 3 weeks. I can then cover up the dug up land with sawdust/ garden rubbish, or concrete over if you'd prefer?

Can you pass me details of anywhere suitable and ill make sure there's a drink in it for you?

Cheers

Pat

**From: Woodlands.co.uk
To: Pat Keriss
Subject: Help**

**Sorry
We cannot help on this
Simon Feltham**

Brett Ellis has asserted his right under the copyright, designs and patents act 1988 to be identified as the author of this work.

This book is a work of non fiction based on the life, experiences and recollections of Brett Ellis aka 'Pat Keriss'. In some limited cases names of people, places, dates, sequences or the detail of events have been changed to protect the privacy of others. The contents of this book are true.

ISBN: 1450522246
EAN-13: 9781450522243

This book is sold subject to the condition that it shall not, by way of trade or otherwise, be lent, resold, hired out, or otherwise circulated without Brett Ellis' prior knowledge in any form of binding or cover other than that in which it is published and without a similar condition, including this condition, being imposed on the subsequent purchaser.

Thankyou for purchasing this book.
I appreciate it.

Brett Ellis
(patkeriss@yahoo.co.uk)

Final word: Many thanks to you for buying this book. To my wife for not moaning too much at the time I spend on my frolics. Love to my baby girl for being the most adorable little munchkin in the whole wide world. To Roger, for spitting coffee on me (twice) whilst reading a selection of e-mails...not the response I expected, but welcome nonetheless. A final hi goes to my friends and family (including Barnsey, Lee, Tony, Peter, Paul x2, Lisa, Lhiam, Niall, Mum, Rita, Scott, Damien and all the others). The book would still have been possible without them, but I would feel guilty not saying hello!

Made in the USA
Charleston, SC
12 April 2010